Betty Crocker's

New Choices for

Pasta, Grains and Beans

MACMILLAN • USA

MACMILLAN

A Prentice Hall Macmillan Company
15 Columbus Circle
New York, New York 10023

Library of Congress Cataloging-in-Publication Data

Crocker, Betty.
[New Choices for pasta, grains & beans cookbook]
Betty Crocker's new choices for pasta, grains & beans cookbook.
p. cm.
Includes index.
ISBN 0-02-860362-1

1. Cookery (pasta)   2. Cookery (Cereals)   3. Cookery (Beans)
I. Title.   II. Title: New choices for pasta, grains & beans cookbook.
III. Title: New choices for pasta, grains & beans cookbook.
TX809.M17C77   1995
641.8'22—dc20   94-24257
CIP

Manufactured in the United States of America

10 9 8 7 6 5 4 3 2 1

First Edition

GENERAL MILLS, INC.

Betty Crocker Food and Publications Center

Director: Marcia Copeland

Editor: Lori Fox

Recipe Development: Jann Atkins, Julie O'Meara and Anne Stuart

Food Stylists: Kate Condon and Cindy Lund

Nutrition Department
Nutritionist: Elyse Cohen and Nancy Holmes

Photographic Services
Photographer: Nancy Doonan Dixon

Preceding page: Smoked Turkey and Couscous, California Club Pasta (page 28)

Contents page: Chilled Shrimp Fettuccine (page 38), Harvest Salad (page 116) and Wild Rice–Corn Muffins (page 115), Succotash Chicken Soup (page 156)

Front Cover: Three-Pepper Pasta (page 62), Apple-Rosemary Pork and Barley (page 80), Mediterranean Salad (page 167)

Back Cover: Nutty Pasta (page 60)

Cover by Iris Jeromnimon
Designed by Michele Laseau

Introduction

Add bold, new excitement to your everyday meals using our creative recipes for pasta, grains and beans. With *Betty Crocker's New Choices for Pasta, Grains and Beans* you can enjoy a wide variety of new meal choices that are both healthy and delicious! Each chapter includes helpful glossaries and photographs identifying the types of pasta, grains and beans, and complete cooking guides with cooking tips.

You'll be delighted by the "pastabilities" of pasta! With so many varieties of pasta available, you could enjoy a different kind each night. Sample Couscous Chicken Waldorf Salad, Spaghetti Torte, Thai Chicken and Broccoli with Spicy Peanut Sauce or Sichuan Pasta Toss.

Next you can enjoy the world of grains—there's so much more than rice! Try new grains such as those in Dilled Corn with Popped Amaranth, Wheat Berry Salad, Quinoa and Artichoke Salad, or traditional Quick Beef Barley Soup.

And finally, you will find out how to use beans other than in baked beans and chili. You'll love Easy Cassoulet, Black Bean Lasagne, Curried Lentils and Rice and Moroccan Vegetables.

With *Betty Crocker's New Choices for Pasta, Grains and Beans* you'll be able to solve the puzzle of how to serve great meals that are also good for you!

Betty Crocker

Contents

Nutrition Symbols

Every one of the delicious recipes in this book meets at least one of the five nutritional criteria shown below; many meet several. See page 21 for more details.

LOW CALORIE

LOW FAT

LOW CHOLESTEROL

LOW SODIUM

HIGH FIBER

Eating Right *6*

If trying to eat healthy seems confusing, then this no-nonsense chapter is just right for you.

1 Pleasing Pasta *23*

Delicious, filling pasta without butter, cream and lots of cheese? Yes! Explore the many enticing "pastabilities," including soups, salads, side dishes and main dishes.

2 Great Grains *73*

In addition to rice, many other grains are equally as versatile and flavorful. Whether it's a creamy cornmeal polenta or a fluffy millet pilaf, you're sure to find many tasty new ideas.

3 Bountiful Beans *123*

The humble bean isn't just for baked beans anymore. From luscious lasagne to terrific sandwiches and soups, beans can really "beef-up" your meals!

Index *172*

Eating Right

There's welcome news today for people interested in healthy eating. Food that's good for you can be enjoyable! What's more, by building nutrition basics into a plan for eating that is delicious and satisfying, you actually increase your chances to permanently improve your healthy eating habits. But you certainly don't have to be a nutrition expert to succeed. This chapter gives you all the information you need to make healthy eating a reality for you and your family.

Cutting Back on Dietary Fat and Cholesterol

It seems hard to find a current magazine that doesn't include an article about how to cut back on dietary fat. Why is this tasty nutrient getting so much attention? Part of the answer lies in the fact that fat tastes good. It provides flavor and contributes to how satisfied you feel after eating a meal. In short, fat's a nutrient that makes foods very appealing, so appealing that we tend to eat too many and too much of foods that contain a high percentage of fat.

Excess fat in the diet, however, has been implicated in the development of some of the major health problems afflicting Americans today, such as heart disease and certain types of cancer. High-fat diets also may contribute to the development of obesity. For healthy eating, we must take care not to overindulge where dietary fat is concerned.

All about Fat

With everything you've read or heard about fat, you may believe it's a good idea to try to eliminate it from your diet. But the truth is we actually need some fat. It is our only source of linoleic acid, a fatty acid essential for proper growth, healthy skin and the proper metabolism of cholesterol.

Also essential is the role fat plays in the transport, absorption and storage of fat-soluble vitamins (A, D, E, K). In addition, fat helps the body use carbohydrates and protein more efficiently. And finally, fat deposits—where much of the body's excess fat is stored—play an important role in insulating and cushioning the body and organs.

On the average, Americans eat about 38 percent of their daily calories in the form of fat. Health and nutrition experts recommend people over the age of twenty reduce fat to an average of 30 percent—less than one-third—of daily calories. In a typical 1800-calorie diet, it means a drop from 75 grams to 60 grams of fat a day.

Recommended Daily Nutrient Levels

Calories	Fat(g)	Saturated Fat (g)
1200	40	13
1500	50	17
1800	60	20
2100	70	23
2400	80	27
2700	90	30
3000	100	33

Although about one-third of all the fat Americans eat comes from meat, fish and poultry, fat from animal sources actually has decreased in the past 40 years. Fourteen percent of the fat we eat is made up of fats such as butter, margarine, mayonnaise, oils and sauces. Mixed dishes such as casseroles, pizza, and lasagna, as well as milk and milk products, each provide 13 percent of total dietary fat.

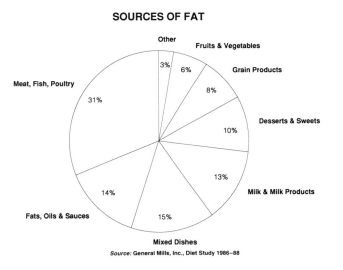

SOURCES OF FAT

Other 3%
Fruits & Vegetables 6%
Grain Products 8%
Desserts & Sweets 10%
Milk & Milk Products 13%
Mixed Dishes 15%
Fats, Oils & Sauces 14%
Meat, Fish, Poultry 31%

Source: General Mills, Inc., Diet Study 1986–88

The pie chart above presents a complete breakdown of dietary fat sources in the average American diet.

Along with limiting the total amount of fat we eat, we're also advised to cut back on how much saturated fat we eat. All dietary fat is made up of mixtures of three types of fatty acids: saturated, monounsaturated and polyunsaturated. Because saturated fat has been linked to high blood cholesterol levels, a major risk factor for coronary heart disease (CHD), it's recommended we reduce our intake of this type of fat to no more than 10 percent of daily calories. In a typical diet, about 13 percent of calories comes from saturated fat.

Animal foods such as meats, eggs and dairy products including cheese, butter and cream contain the greatest amounts of saturated fats. Tropical fats—coconut, palm and palm kernel oils—are unique because they are derived from plant sources, yet they too contain significant amounts of saturated fats.

Saturated fats have a greater effect on blood cholesterol levels than any other dietary factor. As long as total fat intake is still within the suggested range (not more than 30 percent), substituting polyunsaturated or monounsaturated fats such as olive, peanut, corn, soybean and safflower (canola) oils for saturated fats may help lower blood cholesterol.

Not all saturated fatty acids have the same cholesterol-raising potential. Research shows that stearic acid, a saturated fatty acid found in beef and chocolate, does not increase blood cholesterol levels. Palm oil, high in saturated fatty acids, seems to behave differently from other saturated fats, too. However, more research is needed to investigate the long-term effects of these fatty acids on blood cholesterol levels.

The level of saturation of any fat can be changed by hydrogenation. The hydrogenation process changes unsaturated fatty acids to a more saturated—and more stable—chemical structure. Highly unsaturated vegetable oils, for example, are not stable enough for use in packaged foods because they develop "off" flavors in short periods of time. To increase stability, these oils are "saturated" with hydrogen, thereby hydrogenating them and making them more shelf stable.

Typical hydrogenated fats include shortening, which is made by blending hydrogenated vegetable oils to provide desirable physical properties of taste and shelf stability for packaged foods. Vegetable oil margarine becomes solid and spreadable at room temperature as a result of the hydrogenation process.

What about Cholesterol?

In the effort to reduce dietary fat in order to lower blood cholesterol, it's easy to get confused. What about the cholesterol we eat? Where does that fit in?

The cholesterol in the foods we eat is dietary cholesterol. However, the cholesterol in our blood comes from two sources: the foods we eat and the body's own manufacturing process. Dietary cholesterol is found only in animal foods such as meat and milk. For most individuals, dietary cholesterol seems to have minimal influence on blood cholesterol because the body regulates the level.

You may have heard about two other types of cholesterol—"bad" cholesterol, or low-density lipoproteins (LDL), and "good" cholesterol, high-density lipoproteins (HDL). LDLs and HDLs together make up total blood cholesterol along with VLDL (very-low-density lipoprotein). Thought to be the culprit in heart disease, LDL contains most of the cholesterol found in the blood and is associated with making cholesterol available for cell structures, hormones and nerve coverings. LDL deposits cholesterol on artery walls as well. HDL seems to help remove cholesterol from body tissues and blood so it can be recycled and used again. Studies indicate that the more HDL in the blood, the lower the risk for heart disease.

The National Heart, Lung and Blood Institute's National Cholesterol Education Program (NCEP) initially classifies risk for heart disease based on total blood cholesterol levels as follows:

> Under 200 mg/dl*—Desirable
>
> 200–239 mg/dl—Borderline–High
>
> 240 mg/dl or over—High

NCEP recommends that individuals with cholesterol readings of 200 mg/dl and above have another test done to reconfirm the readings. Then, if levels remain borderline–high or above and the individual has two or more risk factors for coronary heart disease (CHD) or has been diagnosed with the disease, lipoprotein levels should be analyzed, particularly the amounts of LDL and HDL. NCEP classifications for LDL and HDL are listed below:

HDL Cholesterol

Under 35 mg/dl—Low

Under 130 mg/dl—Desirable

LDL Cholesterol

Under 130 mg/dl—Desirable

130–159 mg/dl—Borderline–High

160 md/dl or over—High

Milligrams of cholesterol per deciliter of blood.

Major risk factors for CHD include heredity, cigarette smoking, high blood pressure, obesity, physical inactivity and diabetes mellitus. All individuals over the age of twenty with desirable cholesterol levels should have them rechecked every five years.

Like fat, cholesterol is essential to life, so we don't want to eliminate it from our diets. Cholesterol is vital, and our bodies have a built-in safeguard to ensure we get the cholesterol we need. The body makes 800 to 1500 milligrams of cholesterol daily, which circulates through the bloodstream to meet various needs. Among its many important functions, cholesterol is involved in manufacturing certain hormones and is an essential part of the brain and nervous system.

Americans also tend to eat more dietary cholesterol than is recommended. Average intakes run more than 400 milligrams a day; health experts recommend no more than 300 milligrams. The most concentrated sources of dietary cholesterol are organ meats, such as liver, brain and kidney. Egg yolk contains a significant amount of dietary cholesterol too.

What Is Fiber?

Although there is no universal agreement on a definition, fiber is usually described as those components of plant foods that are not broken down in the human digestive tract or absorbed into the blood stream. Fiber is a complex carbohydrate, one of the foods we are encouraged to eat more of as we eat less fat, sugar and cholesterol. Moreover, fiber contributes virtually no calories.

Fiber, part of the structural material in plants, is present in most foods containing complex carbohydrates, such as whole-grain cereals and breads and many vegetables and fruits. Fiber is not found in meat and dairy products.

High-Fiber Foods—Citrus fruits, apples, bananas, pineapple, carrots, potatoes, broccoli, cauliflower, lentils, dried beans, whole grains, corn on the cob, popcorn, whole-grain breads and whole-grain crackers.

Filling Up with Fiber

You don't have to be a scientist to recognize that high-fiber foods go a long way toward helping you feel full and satisfied after a meal. Studies of fiber's effect on appetite control and obesity are now being conducted. Fiber-rich foods take longer to digest and may help tame hunger between meals and even make you less hungry at the next one.

But there's much more to fiber than that. It appears that a high-fiber diet may have a positive effect on cancer of the colon and rectum,

Soluble and Insoluble Fiber Comparisons

Food	Serving Size	Total Dietary Fiber(g)	Amount of Fiber(g) Soluble	Insoluble
Kidney beans	3/4 cup	9.3	2.3	7.0
Oat Bran	1/3 cup	4.0	2.0	2.0
Cheerios®	1 cup	3.0	1.0	2.0
Carrots	1/2 cup	3.2	1.5	1.7
Apple	1 small	2.8	1.0	1.8
Broccoli	1/2 cup	2.8	1.3	1.5
Oatmeal	3/4 cup	2.5	1.2	1.3
Orange	1 medium	1.9	1.1	0.8
Corn	1/2 cup	1.9	0.2	1.7
Cornflake cereal	1 cup	0.5	0.1	0.4

cardiovascular disease and diabetes, in addition to affecting intestinal regularity and diverticular disease.

Many of these beneficial effects are due to the water-holding capacity of one type of fiber called insoluble fiber, especially the insoluble fiber from wheat and corn bran. While this fiber does not dissolve in water, it does have the effect of drawing more water into the intestinal tract and keeping it there. More water means softer, bulkier and heavier stools, which move more quickly through the digestive tract and help prevent constipation.

Furthermore, this water-holding capacity is thought to be one of the chemical properties that influences cancer risk. It may dilute the concentration of carcinogens in the stool and by moving the stool quickly through the intestines, helps reduce the time the intestinal wall is exposed to carcinogens. Another property may be fiber's capacity to bind carcinogens, thus making them unable to affect the body.

Until recently, the other type of fiber—soluble fiber—was ignored largely because its role in the diet was unclear. But it has been shown to have important effects in digestive and absorptive processes and may help control blood sugar levels in people with diabetes mellitus. In addition, research confirms repeatedly that when soluble fiber is included in a low-fat diet, it may help lower blood cholesterol a small but significant amount. This effect seems to be more pronounced in individuals with high levels of blood cholesterol. Some of these benefits may result from the ability of soluble fibers to dissolve in aqueous or watery solutions, thereby forming gels that slow the digestion and absorption of some substances.

Despite these good health benefits, the daily dietary fiber intake of the average American has decreased since the turn of the century. While there is no established Recommended Dietary Allowance (RDA) for dietary fiber, nutrition experts and the Food and Drug Administration currently suggest individuals consume about 25 grams per day as the Daily Value. Larger individuals should consume more fiber than smaller individuals.

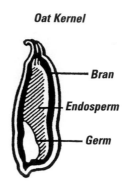

Oat Kernel

Bran

Endosperm

Germ

It's estimated that we now eat 10 to 20 grams of dietary fiber per day. The goal recently established by the National Cancer Institute means, for most Americans, doubling their intake.

Many people are confused about the relationship of bran to dietary fiber. Bran is the coarse, outer layer of the whole-grain kernel and is the source of fiber in the kernel. In addition to fiber, bran contains some starch, protein, a very small amount of fat, and minerals such as iron and zinc. But all bran is not alike. Depending on the grain source of the bran, it will have different amounts of soluble and insoluble fiber (see table on page 9).

Whole-grain cereals are excellent sources of insoluble fiber; it's also found in dried beans and peas, vegetables and nuts. Soluble fiber is perhaps best known in the form of oat bran, but other good sources include whole-grain oats and barley, apples, oranges, dried beans and other legumes. A healthful intake of both insoluble and soluble fiber is recommended. To ensure that, eat a variety of whole grains, vegetables and fruits.

Vital Vitamins and Minerals

Vitamins and minerals are crucial to good health. Vitamins and minerals typically come from the foods we eat, and different foods provide different nutrients—one reason why our diets should be balanced and varied.

Vitamins help to control most body processes. They are important for vision and maintaining healthy tissues such as skin and hair. Vitamins aid our nerve activity and even help our ability to release energy from the foods we eat. They are organic compounds that contain carbon and are found in small amounts in many foods.

Vitamins are classified according to their ability to dissolve in water or fat. Water-soluble vitamins are not retained by the body and must be replenished daily. Fat-soluble vitamins are stored in the fatty tissue of the body and can build up with time. Water-soluble vitamins include thiamin (B_1), riboflavin (B_2), niacin (B_3), B_6, B_{12}, biotin, folic acid, pantothenic acid and vitamin C. Vitamins A, D, E and K are fat-soluble.

Minerals differ from vitamins because they are inorganic, meaning they do not contain the element carbon. Examples of key dietary minerals are calcium, iron, potassium, sodium, phosphorus, magnesium and zinc. Minerals are important for strong bones and teeth, for normal growth, for oxygen transfer in blood and in helping to maintain body water balance.

Boning Up on Calcium

You may already know that healthy bones and teeth depend on getting enough calcium during the growing years. But even as adults, we need to make sure we meet our calcium needs. Calcium plays an important role in the normal functioning of muscles and nerves, blood clotting and various hormonal systems. Plus, current research points to calcium as vital to the prevention and treatment of diseases commonly seen as we grow older such as osteoporosis (weak, brittle bones) and possibly high blood pressure.

Dairy products such as milk and cheese contribute more than half of the calcium consumed in the United States. Other sources include leafy green vegetables such as broccoli, kale and collards,

High-Calcium Foods—Low-fat dairy products (including cheeses, milks, yogurts, frozen yogurt and ice milk), spinach, kale, collard greens, broccoli, dried beans and canned salmon and sardines (with bones).

tortillas processed with lime, tofu made with cal-cium and calcium-fortified foods. The soft bones of fish such as sardines and canned salmon also contain significant amounts of calcium.

For women and men twenty-five years old and older, the RDA for calcium is 800 milligrams per day. The RDA is set at 1200 milligrams for girls and boys between the ages of eleven and twenty-four, and pregnant and nursing women. Recent surveys, however, indicate many Americans do not meet their need for calcium. This is especially worrisome for adolescent girls and adult women, who run the greatest risk of developing osteoporosis.

One reason for this calcium shortfall is the misconception that all dairy foods are high in fat and calories. As a result, many girls and women eliminate dairy foods from their diets to lose or maintain weight. But that isn't necessary to control calories. Many types of reduced-fat milk, cheeses and other dairy products are now available. And they taste good, too, making it easier to meet calcium needs while controlling weight.

Other people cut back on dairy products because they suffer from lactose intolerance, which means they cannot digest lactose (milk sugar). They lack the intestinal enzyme lactase that breaks down lactose so it can be absorbed. As a result, when they drink milk or other dairy foods that contain a lot of lactose, they may become bloated and suffer from cramps and/or diarrhea. The people most often affected include those of African American, Hispanic, Asian, Native American and Mediterranean descent.

Some lactose-intolerant people, however, don't need to eliminate dairy foods from their diets. The symptoms appear to be dose-related, meaning that an individual may be able to tolerate small amounts of dairy foods without developing symptoms. Exactly how much a person can tolerate is quite individual. Some people can drink a whole cup of milk with a meal without experiencing symptoms, while others have problems after drinking very small amounts of milk.

Calcium-Rich Food

Food	Calcium(mg)
Beans, dried, cooked, 1 cup	90
Broccoli, cooked, 1/2 cup	90
Cheese	
American, pasteurized processed, 1 ounce	174
Cottage, 2% low-fat, 1/2 cup	77
Ricotta, part skim, 1/2 cup	337
Cheddar, 1 ounce	204
Mozzarella, part skim, 1 ounce	207
Swiss, 1 ounce	272
Collards, fresh, cooked, 1/2 cup	74
Ice cream, 1/2 cup	88
Ice milk, hardened, 1/2 cup	88
Ice milk, soft serve, 1/2 cup	137
Kale, frozen, cooked, 1/2 cup	90
Milk	
Buttermilk, 1 cup	285
Whole, 1 cup	291
1% low-fat, 1 cup	300
2% low-fat, 1 cup	297
Skim, 1 cup	302
Pudding, chocolate, 1/2 cup	133
Salmon, with bones, 3 ounces	167
Sardines, with bones, 3 ounces	371
Spinach, fresh, cooked, 1/2 cup	122
Tofu, 4 ounces	108
Yogurt	
Low-fat, flavored, 1 cup	389
Low-fat, fruit, 1 cup	345
Low-fat, plain, 1 cup	415

Source: The All-American Guide to Calcium-Rich Foods, National Dairy Council, Rosemont, IL, 1987.

If you suffer from lactose intolerance, you can find your individual tolerance for dairy foods by eating them in small portions, then gradually increasing the portion size until you begin to notice symptoms. Then, don't exceed that portion per serving. To meet your calcium needs, space several servings of dairy products throughout the day.

Symptoms may also be avoided by drinking milk with solid foods rather than drinking it by itself. In addition, lactose-reduced milks are now available in many supermarkets. Also, aged hard cheeses such as Cheddar, Swiss and Parmesan do not cause symptoms for many people, because most of the lactose is removed during processing. Yogurt with active cultures is also well tolerated because the cultures contain enzymes that break down lactose.

Being Sensible about Sodium

Attention to sodium in recent years is due to its link with high blood pressure in some people.

While no single factor causes high blood pressure, experts generally agree that different factors play greater or lesser roles in different people. Some people, it seems, inherit a genetic tendency for high blood pressure that is sodium sensitive. Too much sodium in their diets causes their blood pressure to rise. On the other hand, some people can eat all the sodium they want and seem never to suffer negative effects.

The trouble is, there's no good way to test for sodium sensitivity prior to the actual onset of high blood pressure. The cause of high blood pressure is unknown in the majority of Americans. The word to the wise then, points to moderation in sodium consumption.

As with the other dietary substances we've discussed, sodium is essential. It is needed to regulate

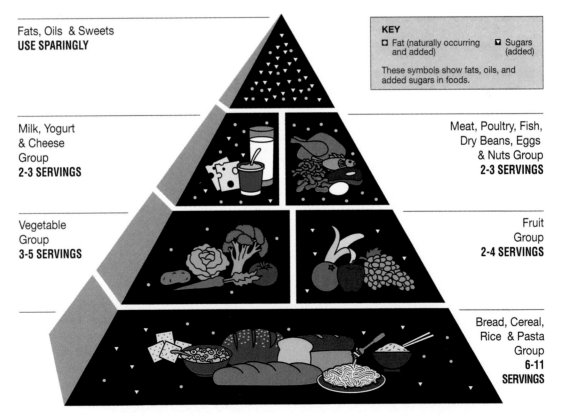

FOOD GUIDE PYRAMID: A Guide to Daily Food Choices

Fats, Oils & Sweets
USE SPARINGLY

KEY
☐ Fat (naturally occurring and added)   ◼ Sugars (added)
These symbols show fats, oils, and added sugars in foods.

Milk, Yogurt & Cheese Group
2-3 SERVINGS

Meat, Poultry, Fish, Dry Beans, Eggs & Nuts Group
2-3 SERVINGS

Vegetable Group
3-5 SERVINGS

Fruit Group
2-4 SERVINGS

Bread, Cereal, Rice & Pasta Group
6-11 SERVINGS

Source: U.S. Department of Agriculture, U.S. Department of Health and Human Services

blood pressure and blood volume and also aids the proper functioning of nerves and muscles. The National Research Council, which sets the RDAs, has established a safe and adequate range of sodium intake for adults at 1,100 to 3,300 milligrams per day. The Food and Drug Administration uses 2,400 mg per day as the Daily Value for sodium. Surveys indicate Americans are in no danger of suffering a shortage of sodium. Estimates of average sodium intake in America range up to 5,000 milligrams a day.

Sodium occurs naturally in a wide variety of foods such as dairy products, eggs, meat, poultry and vegetables. Sodium is added to other foods during processing in the form of ingredients used to enhance flavor or act as preservatives or emulsifiers. Salt is one such ingredient; it is 40 percent sodium and serves a variety of purposes in foods. Other sodium-rich ingredients feature the word *sodium* in their names: monosodium glutamate (a flavor enhancer), sodium benzoate (a preservative), sodium caseinate (a thickener and binder). These names are listed in the ingredient list of packaged foods that contain them. Other sources of sodium include condiments, seasonings and sauces such as soy, steak and barbecue sauces, catsup, relishes and bouillon cubes. Manufacturers today are introducing sodium-reduced versions of many of these items.

Building a Healthful Diet

After reading the preceding pages, you may think our claim that you don't need to be a nutrition expert to eat healthfully isn't true! After all, how can you balance concerns about fat, cholesterol, fiber, calcium and sodium yet still have a food plan that includes foods you love and have eaten all your life?

It's actually fairly easy if you take it one step at a time. Approach it as though you're building a house (in a sense, you are—you're building your body for a long, healthy life). Start with a good, solid foundation. The foundation of a nutritious diet is a wide variety of foods. You need more than 40 different nutrients to maintain good health, and no single food supplies them all in the necessary amounts. And that's just as well because it would be boring to eat just one item day after day. Much of the pleasure of food comes from enjoying the flavors and textures of the wonderful assortment of items available to us today.

To best ensure you meet both your nutrient and pleasure requirements, select a wide variety of foods from the Food Pyramid Guide (page 13). Choose low-fat items most of the time but when you wish, you can occasionally enjoy higher-fat, higher-calorie items too.

Eat at least the minimum recommended number of servings from each food group daily. Whether you eat more depends on your individual needs. For example, if you exercise regularly, you may require more servings from each group in order to maintain your weight. If you're unsure of how to handle your new food plan, a registered dietitian can help decide what is best for you.

When planning meals, remember the special nutrient concerns discussed earlier. To control fat, saturated fat and cholesterol, select more plant foods, such as cereals, rice, pasta and beans. Use meat, poultry and fish as "flavor enhancers" rather than the main feature of meals. Use fats and oils sparingly in cooking.

To increase fiber, choose whole-grain cereals and breads, brown rice and dried peas or beans. Serve fruits and vegetables unpeeled. Meet your calcium needs with a wide variety of reduced-fat dairy products. And be wise about sodium by carefully managing the amount of high-sodium foods you eat and how much salt you add to foods during cooking or at the table. Learn to enjoy the natural flavors of foods; enhance flavors with spices and herbs and a small amount of salt only when necessary.

The Framework— a Healthy Attitude

The framework for your healthy body is formed by your attitude about eating and exercise. How you approach making changes, your ideas about weight management and how you manage special eating occasions all combine to help you decide whether your initial changes become permanent. There is always room for adjustment.

Lasting changes are truly important. Fluctuation back and forth between old and new habits may not only prevent you from ever reaching your goals, but can even cause harm. For instance, constantly losing and regaining weight may end up adding to health problems rather than helping to alleviate them. As a result, experts today support an approach to improving eating and exercise habits that recognizes individual needs.

Gone are the days of preprinted diet and exercise plans. For long-term effectiveness, individual desires, obstacles and issues must be addressed. In short, the approach must be realistic, practical and tailored to each individual. Furthermore, experts advise a slow start to building new habits. If you're a couch potato who skips breakfast and lunch, then starts eating the moment you get home from work and doesn't stop until your head hits the pillow, you're not likely to succeed if you try to totally revamp your diet and begin training for marathons at the same time. A better way, and one that is more manageable, is to focus on two or three major eating or exercise habits. For example, you may decide to start eating breakfast and focus on reducing after-dinner snacking. And you might set a goal for three 20-minute walks a week. When you achieve those goals, you can address other areas you think need improvement. Nothing succeeds better than success, so set yourself up to win by defining small, achievable goals along the way to your overall goal.

Going slowly where weight is concerned is vital, too. The best approach to managing your weight is to eat moderately following the Food Guide

Suggested Healthy Weights for Adults

| | Weight (lbs)** | |
Height*	Age 19 to 34 years	Age 35 years and over
5′0″	†97–128	108–138
5′1″	101–132	111–143
5′2″	104–137	115–148
5′3″	107–141	119–152
5′4″	111–146	122–157
5′5″	114–150	126–162
5′6″	118–155	130–167
5′7″	121–160	134–172
5′8″	125–164	138–178
5′9″	129–169	142–183
5′10″	132–174	146–188
5′11″	136–179	151–194
6′0″	140–184	155–199
6′1″	144–189	159–205
6′2″	148–195	164–210
6′3″	152–200	168–216
6′4″	156–205	173–222
6′5″	160–211	177–228
6′6″	164–216	182–234

Without shoes.

**Without clothes.*

† The higher weights in the ranges generally apply to men, who tend to have more muscle and bone; the lower weights more often apply to women, who have less muscle and bone.

Source: *Nutrition and Your Health: Dietary Guidelines for Americans,* Third Edition, 1990, U.S. Department of Agriculture, U.S. Department of Health and Human Services, Washington, D.C.

Pyramid and to exercise regularly. Quick weight-loss schemes, particularly those that advise eliminating any food group, can jeopardize both your nutritional status and your chances for success at weight management.

An effective approach to weight management also considers "healthy" weights. Healthy weights

Calories Burned in Various Physical Activities

Activity	Calories per Minute	Activity	Calories per Minute	Activity	Calories per Minute
Aerobics		Gymnastics		Reclining	
low-intensity	3.0–4.0	balancing	2.5	(watching TV)	1.5
high-intensity	8.0–10.0	abdominal	3.0	Roller skating	
Archery	5.2	trunk bending	3.5	(moderate to	
Badminton		hopping	6.5	vigorous)	5.0–15.0
recreation	5.2	Handball	10.0	Rowing	
competition	10.0	Hiking		pleasure	5.0
Baseball		downhill, 5–10		vigorous	15.0
(except pitcher)	4.7	percent grade		Running	
Basketball		(2.5 mph)	3.5–3.6	12-minute mile	
half court	6.0	downhill, 15–20		(5 mph)	9.0
fastbreak	9.0	percent grade		8-minute mile	
Bowling		(2.5 mph)	3.7–4.3	(7.5 mph)	11.0
(while active)	7.0	road/field		6-minute mile	
Calisthenics	6.0–8.0	(3.5 mph)	5.6–7.0	(10 mph)	20.0
Canoeing		snow, soft-hard		5-minute mile	
(2.5–4.0 mph)	3.0–7.0	(2.5–3.5 mph)	10.0–20.0	(12 mph)	25.0
Carpentry	3.8	uphill, 5–15		Sawing	
Cleaning windows	3.7	percent grade		chain saw	6.2
Clerical work	1.2–1.6	(3.5 mph)	8.0–15.6	crosscut saw	7.5–10.5
Cycling		Hill climbing (100		Sewing (hand or	
fast (12 mph)	8.0–10.0	feet/hour)	8.2	machine)	0.6
slow (6 mph)	4.0–5.0	Hockey	12.0–15.0	Shining shoes	3.2
10-speed bicycle		Horseback riding		Shoveling (depends on	
(5–15 mph)	4.0–12.0	trot	5.0	weight of load,	
Dancing (moderate		walk	1.6	rate of work,	
to vigorous)	4.2–7.7	Horseshoes	3.8	height of lift)	5.4–10.5
Dishwashing	1.2	Ironing clothes	4.2	Showering	3.4
Dressing	3.4	Jogging alternated		Singing in loud voice	0.9
Driving car	2.8	with walking,		Sitting quietly	0.5
Driving motorcycle	3.4	5 minutes each	10.0	Skipping rope	10.0–15.0
Dusting	2.5	Judo and karate	13.0	Skiing (snow)	
Eating	2.5	Knitting or crocheting	0.5–0.8	moderate to steep	8.0–12.0
Farming chores		Making beds	3.4	downhill racing	16.5
haying	6.7	Meal preparation	2.5	cross-country	
planting	4.7	Mopping floors	4.9	(3.8 mph)	11.0–20.0
Football (while active)	13.3	Mountain climbing	10.0	Sleeping	0.5–1.2
Gardening		Piano playing	1.6	Snowshoeing (2.5 mph)	10.0
digging	8.6	Plastering walls	4.1	Soccer	9.0
weeding	5.6	Pool or billiards	1.8	Standing, light	
Golf		Racquetball		activity	2.6
foursome	2.7	recreation	8.1	Standing, relaxed	0.6
twosome	3.0	competition	11.5		

Calories Burned in Various Physical Activities *(continued)*

Activity	Calories per Minute	Activity	Calories per Minute	Activity	Calories per Minute
Sweeping with:		Table tennis	5.1	Walking	
broom	1.6	Talking	1.0–1.2	3 mph	4.0–5.0
vacuum cleaner	3.2	Tennis		4 mph	6.0–7.0
Swimming		recreation	7.0	downstairs	4.0
pleasure	6.0	competition	11.0	upstairs	8.0–10.0
backstroke,		Tree felling (ax)	8.4–12.7	Washing and	
breaststroke		Truck and auto		dressing	2.6
crawl (25–50		repair	4.2	Washing clothes	3.1
yard/minute)	6.0–12.5	Typing (rapidly)	1.2	Water skiing	8.0
butterfly (50		Volleyball		Wrestling	14.4
yard/minute)	14.0	recreation	3.5	Writing	0.5
		competition	8.0		

depend on the individual, and for some people, that's far from the super-slim-fashion-model image popular today. Indeed, you may be healthy at a higher weight than your neighbor, even though you both are the same height. A realistic approach allows for a small amount of weight gain, maybe a few extra pounds, as we age.

Two simple measures of healthy weight include determining where excess fat is located (it's considered a greater health risk if fat is found primarily on the abdomen) and if you or your family has a history of health problems that may be aggravated by excess weight, such as diabetes or heart disease. Check to see if your weight falls within a healthy range as defined in the table on the left.

Being realistic during the food-filled holidays and other special celebrations is important as well. At those times, it seems that tasty, high-fat, high-calorie tidbits lurk in every corner, just waiting to sabotage our efforts. But there's really no need to throw in the towel at these times. You can have your cake and eat it, too. All it takes is a little planning.

It helps tremendously to remember that healthful eating depends on balance, variety and moderation. All foods can fit within a healthy diet; what's important is how often and how much you eat of certain foods. To successfully navigate special occa-

sions anticipate meals high in fat or cholesterol. Offset them by eating low-fat, low-cholesterol foods the days before and after.

Remember, too, that one mistake does not destroy all your good efforts. If you overeat—for one meal, one day or even one week—you can still salvage your healthy eating efforts by returning to your plan. Compare this behavior with totally giving up because you've made a mistake, and you can see that over time you're more likely to reach your goals. Use the Good Eating Guide (pages 18–19) to help you select foods you enjoy that are also healthy. This keeps your eating plan pleasurable and varied.

Finally, any discussion of healthful habits must include a word about exercise. Physical inactivity places more Americans at risk for CHD—our number one killer today—than any other factor. Although a slightly greater risk for the disease comes from cigarette smoking, high blood cholesterol or high blood pressure, the number of Americans who are physically inactive actually exceeds the number who face these other risks. Yet we really don't give exercise the attention it deserves when it comes to its ability to improve and protect our health.

The good news is that we're not necessarily talking about running marathons. Increasing evidence

Good Eating Guide

	Recommended Serving Size	Eat Any Time	Eat in Moderation	Eat Occasionally
Breads/Cereals (6 to 11 servings daily. Includes whole grain, enriched breads and cereals, pasta, rice and crackers.)	1 to 1 1/2 ounces ready-to-eat cereal (varies if it contains fruits, nuts) 1/2 cup cooked cereal, pasta or rice 1 slice bread 1/2 hamburger or hot dog bun 1/2 English muffin or bagel 1 small roll or muffin 1/2 pita (6 inches in diameter) 3 to 4 small or 2 large crackers 2 breadsticks (4 × 1/2 inch) 1 tortilla (6 inches in diameter) 3 cups popcorn 2 medium cookies	Whole grain* or fortified breakfast cereal Whole grain* or enriched bread, rolls, bagels, English muffins, tortillas, low-fat crackers Brown or enriched white rice Whole grain or enriched pasta Plain popcorn, pretzels and low-fat cookies (such as fig bars) and cake (angel food)	Biscuits Bread stuffing Corn bread Muffins and other quick breads Pancakes, waffles Popcorn made with added fat Taco shells	High-fat crackers Croissants Doughnuts Sweet rolls Snack chips (potato chips, corn chips, etc.) Most cookies and cakes
Fruits/Vegetables (5 to 9 servings daily. Include at least one serving citrus or other choice high in Vitamin C daily. Include orange or leafy, dark green vegtables 3 to 4 times a week.)	1 medium fruit such as apple, orange, banana 1/2 grapefruit 3/4 cup juice 1 medium wedge melon 1/2 cup berries 1/4 cup dried fruit 1/2 cup cooked or canned fruit or vegetable 1 medium potato 10 French-fried potatoes (2 to 3 1/2 inches long) 1/2 cup raw chopped vegetables 1 cup leafy raw vegetables, such as spinach 1/8 medium avocado	All fresh, canned or frozen fruits and fruit juices All fresh, canned or frozen vegetables and vegetable juices Plain potato or potato with low-fat topping (such as yogurt)	Vegetables with added butter or margarine Potatoes topped with butter, sour cream or sauces	Fruit pies Deep-fried vegetables French-fried potatoes Vegetables in cream or cheese sauce

Good Eating Guide (*continued*)

	Recommended Serving Size	Eat Any Time	Eat in Moderation	Eat Occasionally
Meats/Protein (2 to 3 servings with a total of about 6 ounces daily.Includes meat, fish, poultry and eggs. Dried beans, peas and nuts are alternatives.)	2 ounces beef (maximum 3 ounces of beef daily) 2 ounces poultry or fish 4 ounces tofu Count the following as 1 ounce of meat: 1 egg (maximum 3 eggs weekly); 3 egg whites; 2 tablespoons peanut butter or whole nuts or seeds; 1/2 cup cooked beans, peas or lentils.	Beef: Lean beef including round, sirloin, chuck and loin Pork: Lean cuts including ham and tenderloin Veal: All trimmed cuts except ground Poultry: All poultry without skin Fish: All fresh and frozen fin fish or shellfish Other: Egg whites, all beans, peas and lentils	Beef: Most cuts including all ground beef, short ribs, corned beef brisket Pork: Most cuts including chops, loin roast Poultry: All poultry with skin Other: Fat-free or low-fat luncheon meats**, peanut butter and other nuts or seeds Eggs: Limit to 3 eggs per week	Beef: USDA prime-grade cuts and heavily marbled cuts Pork: Spareribs, ground pork Lamb: Ground lamb Fish: Fried fish Other: Luncheon meats**, sausages**, frankfurters**, bacon**
Milk/Dairy (2 servings daily. 3 for pregnant or breast-feeding women, 4 for pregnant or breast-feeding teenagers. Includes milk, yogurt, cheese, cottage cheese and pudding).	1 cup milk 1 cup yogurt 1 1/2 ounces cheese 1 cup pudding 1 1/2 cup ice cream, ice milk or low-fat yogurt 2 cups cottage cheese	Skim milk 1% low-fat milk Low-fat buttermilk** Plain nonfat or low-fat yogurt Low-fat cheeses	2% low-fat milk Part-skim milk cheese** Ice milk	Whole-milk, cream, half-and-half Whole milk yogurt All regular cheese** such as American, Cheddar, Brie, etc. Cream cheese and sour cream

*Good source of fiber
**For those who need to limit sodium intake, these foods may be high in sodium (read nutrition labels for sodium content).

suggests that light to moderate physical activity can have significant health benefits, including a decreased risk of CHD. For inactive people, even relatively small increases in activity are associated with measurable health benefits. In addition, light to moderate physical activity is more readily adopted and maintained than vigorous physical activity.

As a result, experts today emphasize light to moderate physical activity as the goal for many Americans. Such activity requires sustained, rhythmic muscular movements and is performed at less than 60 percent of maximum heart rate for your age (subtract your age from 220 to get your maximum heart rate). Examples of such activity include walking, swimming, cycling, dancing, gardening, yardwork and even running after young children! (See chart on pages 16–17.)

In short, today's advice for adopting healthy lifestyles is to be flexible. A flexible approach to healthy living forms a basic structure that can withstand the assaults of individual strengths and weaknesses. It allows us to live happily and healthily every day.

NUTRITION GLOSSARY

Have you been confused by the terms used by nutrition and health experts? Consult this list for explanations of some key words.

Nutrients Substances necessary for life and to build, repair and maintain body cells. Nutrients include protein, carbohydrates, fat, water, vitamins and minerals.

Vitamins Essential substances, found in small amounts in many foods, necessary for controlling body processes. Vitamins, unlike minerals, are organic compounds containing carbon. Vitamins include vitamin A, B vitamins (such as thiamin, niacin, riboflavin) and vitamin C, among others.

Minerals Essential elements other than carbon, hydrogen, oxygen and nitrogen, nutritionally necessary in very small amounts. Minerals are inorganic elements, such as calcium and iron, and are found in our foods and water.

Protein Vital for life and provides energy and structural support of body cells and is also important for growth. Made from amino-acid building blocks that contain nitrogen.

Carbohydrate Key human energy source. All simple sugars and complex carbohydrates (starches) fit into this category.

Fat Provides energy—more than twice the amount supplied by an equal quantity of carbohydrate or protein. Also provides essential nutrients, insulation and protection of body organs.

Saturated Fat Primarily found in animal foods, this type of fat is solid at room temperature. Diets high in saturated fats have been linked to higher blood cholesterol levels, however, not all saturated fats have the same blood cholesterol-raising potential.

Unsaturated fat Found most commonly in plant foods, this type of fat is usually liquid at room temperature. Unsaturated fats may be monounsaturated or polyunsaturated. A laboratory process called hydrogenation is used to alter the chemical structure of unsaturated fats, making them saturated and more shelf stable.

Cholesteral Essential fatlike substance found in animal foods that is needed by the body for hormones to function properly. Our bodies also make cholesterol.

LDL Low-density lipoprotein. Often tagged the "bad" cholesterol, low-density lipoprotein cholesterol travels through the bloodstream depositing cholesterol on artery walls, and making cholesterol available for cell structures, hormones and nerve coverings.

HDL High-density lipoprotein. This type of cholesterol helps to remove cholesterol from body tissues and blood and return it to the liver to be used again. This recycling process has earned it the reputation of "good" cholesterol.

Dietary fiber Often described as the components of plant foods that are not broken down or absorbed by the human digestive tract. Fiber is a complex carbohydrate based on its chemical structure.

Additive Substance added to food to perform certain functions, such as to add color or flavor, prevent spoilage, add nutritional value, or improve texture or consistency.

Food Guide Pyramid Newly developed nutrition educational guide from the U.S. Department of Health and Human Services to teach people about foods and the recommended number of servings from each food group in order to maintain a balanced and healthy diet. It replaces the former Four Basic Food Groups. (See diagram on page 13.)

% U.S. RDA Percentage of United States Recommended Daily Allowance was developed as a relative standard for nutrition labeling of protein, vitamins and minerals on foods and drugs. It is based on the needs of healthy people of various ages and is generally the highest recommended level of each nutrient for all age groups.

% Daily Value Developed by the Food and Drug Administration to replace the % U.S. RDA on nutrition labels. They are based on the average needs of most healthy adults.

CHD Coronary Heart Disease. High blood cholesterol levels and build-up of fatlike plaques that limits the flow of blood to body tissues on the lining of artery walls that may cause tissue damage (heart attack, stroke in the brain) and death. Risk factors include family history of CHD, smoking, high blood pressure and lack of exercise. Dietary guidelines, exercise and/or drug treatment are usually warranted. Also called atherosclerosis.

Nutrition Symbols

You may find it hard to believe that every one of the delicious recipes in this book meets at least one of the five nutritional criteria described at right; many meet several. It is unrealistic to expect each dish, or even each meal, to meet all nutritional needs or guidelines. The introduction to this book, "Eating Right," gives you the information you need to use the nutrition analysis provided with each recipe to put together a healthy eating plan for yourself or your family.

 Low Calorie
Recipes have 350 or fewer calories per serving.

 Low Fat
Recipes have 3 or fewer grams of fat per serving.

 Low Cholesterol
Recipes have 20 or fewer milligrams of cholesterol per serving.

 Low Sodium
Recipes have 140 or fewer milligrams of sodium per serving.

 High Fiber
Recipes have 3 or more grams of fiber per serving.

1
Pleasing Pasta

Garden Fresh Primavera (page 50)

Chicken and Mushroom Linguine

6 SERVINGS

❦

This restaurant favorite is easy to make at home— and just as delicious!

Alfredo Sauce (page 71)

12 ounces uncooked linguine

1 pound skinless, boneless chicken breasts, cut into 1-inch pieces

3 cups sliced mushrooms (about 8 ounces)

1 small onion, chopped (about 1/4 cup)

2 tablespoons chopped fresh parsley

Prepare Alfredo Sauce as directed—except reserve 2 tablespoons freshly grated Parmesan cheese; set aside. Cook and drain linguine as directed on package.

While linguine is cooking, spray 10-inch skillet with nonstick cooking spray. Cook chicken, mushrooms and onion in skillet over medium heat 5 to 7 minutes, stirring occasionally, until chicken is no longer pink in center. Stir in Alfredo Sauce. Toss linguine and chicken mixture. Sprinkle with reserved Parmesan cheese and the parsley.

1 Serving		% Daily Value:	
Calories	425	Vitamin A	14%
Calories from fat	70	Vitamin C	6%
Fat, g	8	Calcium	24%
Saturated, g	2	Iron	26%
Cholesterol, mg	45		
Sodium, mg	510		
Carbohydrate, g	60		
Dietary Fiber, g	4		
Protein, g	32		

Chicken Florentine

4 SERVINGS

❦

This is a great recipe for casual entertaining. Try serving it on a shallow platter with your favorite herb as a pretty garnish.

1/2 cup nonfat Italian dressing

1 tablespoon Italian seasoning

1 pound skinless, boneless chicken breast halves

Alfredo Sauce (page 71)

1 package (10 ounces) frozen chopped spinach, thawed and squeezed to drain

12 ounces uncooked fettuccine

1 tablespoon olive or vegetable oil

Mix dressing and Italian seasoning in large glass or plastic bowl; add chicken, turning to coat. Cover and refrigerate 20 minutes. Meanwhile, prepare Alfredo Sauce as directed—except omit nutmeg. Stir spinach into sauce.

Cook and drain fettuccine as directed on package. While fettuccine is cooking, heat oil in 10-inch nonstick skillet over medium-high heat. Remove chicken from marinade. Cook chicken in oil 7 to 10 minutes, turning once, until juice is no longer pink when centers of thickest pieces are cut. Toss fettuccine and spinach mixture. Place fettuccine on serving platter. Top with chicken and sauce.

1 Serving		% Daily Value:	
Calories	605	Vitamin A	58%
Calories from fat	160	Vitamin C	6%
Fat, g	18	Calcium	42%
Saturated, g	5	Iron	32%
Cholesterol, mg	140		
Sodium, mg	760		
Carbohydrate, g	72		
Dietary Fiber, g	6		
Protein, g	45		

Chicken Florentine

Thai Chicken and Broccoli with Spicy Peanut Sauce

6 SERVINGS

8 ounces uncooked vermicelli

1 pound skinless, boneless chicken breasts, cut into 1/2-inch slices

1 tablespoon lime juice

1 teaspoon curry powder

1 teaspoon grated gingerroot

1 clove garlic, crushed

2 teaspoons chile oil

2 cups broccoli flowerets

1 tablespoon all-purpose flour

1/2 cup evaporated skimmed milk

1 container (8 ounces) vanilla nonfat yogurt (1 cup)

3 tablespoons reduced-fat creamy peanut butter

2 tablespoons low-sodium soy sauce

1/4 to 1/2 teaspoon ground red pepper (cayenne)

1/2 teaspoon coconut extract

2 tablespoons cocktail peanuts, finely chopped

Cook and drain vermicelli as directed on package. While vermicelli is cooking, toss chicken, lime juice, curry powder, gingerroot, garlic and 1 teaspoon of the oil. Heat remaining 1 teaspoon oil in 12-inch nonstick skillet over medium-high heat. Cook chicken mixture and broccoli in oil 5 to 7 minutes, stirring frequently, until chicken is no longer pink in center. Remove mixture from skillet; keep warm.

Mix flour, milk, yogurt, peanut butter, soy sauce, red pepper and coconut flavoring in same skillet. Cook over medium heat 3 to 4 minutes, stirring occasionally, until mixture begins to thicken. Toss vermicelli and sauce. Top with chicken mixture. Sprinkle with peanuts.

1 Serving		% Daily Value:	
Calories	365	Vitamin A	10%
Calories from fat	90	Vitamin C	24%
Fat, g	10	Calcium	16%
Saturated, g	2	Iron	18%
Cholesterol, mg	45		
Sodium, mg	480		
Carbohydrate, g	44		
Dietary Fiber, g	3		
Protein, g	28		

Spring Chicken Pasta

6 SERVINGS

8 ounces uncooked spaghetti

1 pound asparagus, cut into 2-inch pieces

8 sun-dried tomato halves (not oil-packed), chopped

2 cloves garlic, finely chopped

1 1/2 cups chopped yellow bell pepper (about 1 1/2 medium)

3/4 cup chopped red onion (about 1 medium)

1 can (14 1/2 ounces) 1/3-less-salt clear chicken broth

1 1/2 pounds skinless, boneless chicken breasts, cut into 1/2-inch strips

3/4 cup nonfat ricotta cheese

1/3 cup chopped fresh basil leaves

2 tablespoons nonfat sour cream

1/2 teaspoon salt

1/4 teaspoon pepper

Cook and drain spaghetti as directed on package. Cook asparagus, tomatoes, garlic, bell pepper, onion and broth in 3-quart saucepan over medium heat 5 minutes. Stir in chicken. Cook 2 to 3 minutes, stirring constantly, until asparagus is crisp-tender and chicken is no longer pink in center. Stir in spaghetti and remaining ingredients.

1 Serving		% Daily Value:	
Calories	335	Vitamin A	20%
Calories from fat	45	Vitamin C	42%
Fat, g	5	Calcium	12%
Saturated, g	1	Iron	18%
Cholesterol, mg	70		
Sodium, mg	550		
Carbohydrate, g	39		
Dietary Fiber, g	3		
Protein, g	36		

Chicken Spaghetti

6 SERVINGS

1 cup water

1 tablespoon chopped fresh or 1 teaspoon dried oregano leaves

2 teaspoons chopped fresh or 3/4 teaspoon dried basil leaves

1 1/2 teaspoons chopped fresh or 1/2 teaspoon dried marjoram leaves

1 teaspoon sugar

3/4 teaspoon chopped fresh or 1/4 teaspoon dried rosemary leaves

1 large onion, chopped (about 1 cup)

1 clove garlic, crushed

1 bay leaf

1 can (8 ounces) tomato sauce

1 can (6 ounces) tomato paste

1 1/2 cups cut-up cooked chicken

4 cups hot cooked spaghetti

Heat all ingredients except chicken and spaghetti to boiling in 10-inch skillet; reduce heat. Cover and simmer 30 minutes, stirring occasionally. Stir in chicken. Cover and simmer 30 minutes longer, stirring occasionally. Remove bay leaf. Serve sauce over spaghetti.

1 Serving		% Daily Value:	
Calories	230	Vitamin A	10%
Calories from fat	25	Vitamin C	14%
Fat, g	3	Calcium	4%
Saturated, g	1	Iron	18%
Cholesterol, mg	30		
Sodium, mg	610		
Carbohydrate, g	38		
Dietary Fiber, g	3		
Protein, g	16		

California Club Pasta

6 SERVINGS

⧗ ♥ ⧖

3 cups uncooked medium pasta shells (about 8 ounces)

1/2 cup nonfat mayonnaise or salad dressing

1/4 cup nonfat buttermilk

1/2 teaspoon celery salt

1/4 teaspoon freshly ground pepper

1 medium tomato, chopped (about 3/4 cup)

4 ounces deli-style sliced reduced-fat ham, cut into 1/2-inch strips

4 ounces deli-style sliced reduced-fat turkey, cut into 1/2-inch strips

1/4 cup sliced green onions (2 to 3 medium)

6 cups spinach leaves

1/2 avocado, cut into 8 wedges

2 slices reduced-sodium bacon, crisply cooked and crumbled

Cook and drain pasta as directed on package. Rinse with cold water; drain. Mix mayonnaise, buttermilk, celery salt and pepper in large bowl. Add pasta, tomato, ham, turkey and onions; toss.

Place spinach on serving platter. Top with pasta mixture and avocado. Sprinkle with bacon.

1 Serving		% Daily Value:	
Calories	268	Vitamin A	50%
Calories from fat	70	Vitamin C	44%
Fat, g	8	Calcium	8%
Saturated, g	1	Iron	22%
Cholesterol, mg	20		
Sodium, mg	930		
Carbohydrate, g	37		
Dietary Fiber, g	3		
Protein, g	15		

Smoked Turkey and Couscous

4 SERVINGS

⧗

1 can (14 1/2 ounces) 1/3-less-salt clear chicken broth

2 cups broccoli flowerets

1 cup cut-up fully cooked smoked turkey (about 6 ounces)

1 1/2 teaspoons chopped fresh or 1/2 teaspoon dried tarragon leaves

1/2 cup uncooked couscous

1/2 cup shredded reduced-fat Cheddar cheese (2 ounces)

Heat broth to boiling in 10-inch skillet. Stir in broccoli, turkey and tarragon. Cover and cook 3 to 4 minutes or until broccoli is crisp-tender. Stir in couscous; remove from heat. Cover and let stand about 5 minutes or until liquid is absorbed.

Fluff couscous mixture with fork. Sprinkle with cheese. Cover and let stand 3 to 5 minutes or until cheese is melted.

1 Serving		% Daily Value:	
Calories	215	Vitamin A	8%
Calories from fat	55	Vitamin C	34%
Fat, g	6	Calcium	14%
Saturated, g	3	Iron	8%
Cholesterol, mg	45		
Sodium, mg	300		
Carbohydrate, g	21		
Dietary Fiber, g	2		
Protein, g	21		

Smoked Turkey and Couscous, California Club Pasta

Fiery Fettuccine

4 SERVINGS

The spicy flavors of Cajun cooking are highlighted in this innovative pasta. For folks who'd like extra "kick," serve hot red pepper sauce or crushed red pepper flakes on the side.

8 ounces uncooked fettuccine

2 1/2 cups evaporated skimmed milk

2 tablespoons all-purpose flour

1 tablespoon Creole or Cajun seasoning

1 jar (7 ounces) roasted red bell peppers, drained

1/2 pound reduced-fat turkey Italian sausage links, cooked and cut into 1/2-inch pieces

2 green onions, sliced

Cook and drain fettuccine as directed on package. While fettuccine is cooking, place milk, flour, seasoning and peppers in blender or food processor. Cover and blend until smooth.

Pour pepper mixture into 12-inch nonstick skillet. Cook over medium heat, stirring occasionally, until mixture thickens. Stir in sausage; heat through but do not boil. Serve sausage mixture over fettuccine. Sprinkle with onions.

1 Serving		% Daily Value:	
Calories	420	Vitamin A	36%
Calories from fat	65	Vitamin C	52%
Fat, g	7	Calcium	50%
Saturated, g	1	Iron	22%
Cholesterol, mg	90		
Sodium, mg	980		
Carbohydrate, g	61		
Dietary Fiber, g	4		
Protein, g	32		

Couscous–Chicken Waldorf Salad

4 SERVINGS

1 1/2 cups cold cooked couscous

1 cup cut-up cooked chicken (about 6 ounces)

1/2 cup seedless green grapes, cut in half

1/4 cup thinly sliced green onions (2 to 3 medium)

1 medium unpeeled apple, chopped (about 1 cup)

1 medium stalk celery, thinly sliced (about 1/2 cup)

1/2 cup low-fat honey-Dijon dressing

1 teaspoon lemon juice

Mix all ingredients except dressing and lemon juice in large bowl. Mix dressing and lemon juice. Pour over couscous mixture; toss.

1 Serving		% Daily Value:	
Calories	220	Vitamin A	2%
Calories from fat	65	Vitamin C	12%
Fat, g	7	Calcium	4%
Saturated, g	2	Iron	6%
Cholesterol, mg	30		
Sodium, mg	350		
Carbohydrate, g	27		
Dietary Fiber, g	2		
Protein, g	14		

Caribbean Sausage and Peppers

6 SERVINGS

✕ ♈

3 cups uncooked penne pasta (about 8 ounces)

1 teaspoon olive or vegetable oil

1/2 pound fully cooked reduced-fat turkey kielbasa sausage, cut into 1/2-inch pieces

1/2 medium green bell pepper, sliced (about 1 cup)

1/2 medium red bell pepper, sliced (about 1 cup)

1 medium onion, sliced (about 1 cup)

1 tablespoon all-purpose flour

1 tablespoon chopped fresh cilantro

1/4 teaspoon ground cloves

1 mango or peach, cut into 1/2-inch pieces (about 1 cup)

2 cans (14 1/2 ounces each) no-salt-added whole tomatoes, undrained

Cook and drain pasta as directed on package. While pasta is cooking, heat oil in 12-inch non-stick skillet over medium heat. Cook sausage, bell peppers and onion in oil, stirring occasionally, until onion is tender. Stir in flour, cilantro, cloves, mango and tomatoes, breaking up tomatoes. Simmer uncovered 10 minutes. Serve over pasta.

1 Serving		% Daily Value:	
Calories	260	Vitamin A	30%
Calories from fat	55	Vitamin C	50%
Fat, g	6	Calcium	6%
Saturated, g	1	Iron	18%
Cholesterol, mg	55		
Sodium, mg	520		
Carbohydrate, g	43		
Dietary Fiber, g	5		
Protein, g	13		

TEN MINUTE PASTABILITIES

◠◡

1. Use any form of fresh pasta, or use thin dried noodles, such as capellini or vermicelli; they cook the fastest.

2. While the pasta is cooking, mix the ingredients to toss with or serve over the pasta.

3. Toss pasta with bite-size pieces of leftover cooked chicken, beef, or pork, or toss with canned tuna, chicken, ham or salmon.

4. Toss pasta with salads from the deli, such as coleslaw, marinated vegetables or a creamy seafood salad.

5. Top pasta with cut-up vegetables from a salad bar. Use them raw, or cook them in the microwave until crisp-tender. Increase the flavor with a little of your favorite salad dressing.

6. Toss noodles with flavored oils, such as Chinese chile oil, garlic oil or an herb or nut-flavored oil.

7. Toss pasta with roasted bell peppers found in jars or oil-packed sun-dried tomatoes.

8. Use refrigerated pasta sauces or pesto or jars of spaghetti sauce to top pasta. Heat as directed while the pasta is cooking.

9. Toss hot pasta with margarine, butter or olive oil and chopped fresh herbs, then sprinkle with your favorite grated cheese.

10. Make a creamy pasta sauce by pureeing heated undrained stewed tomatoes with a little ricotta or cottage cheese and fresh or dried herbs, such as basil, oregano and chives.

Gingered Beef Lo Mein

6 SERVINGS

❎

Chile oil is vegetable oil that has been steeped or infused with hot chilies. It adds a hot, spicy "kick" to this recipe.

1 cup water

3 tablespoons cornstarch

1 tablespoon packed brown sugar

3 tablespoons low-sodium soy sauce

2 teaspoons grated gingerroot

1 teaspoon low-sodium beef bouillon granules

4 ounces uncooked vermicelli

2 teaspoons chile oil

1 pound beef boneless sirloin steak, cut into 2 × 1/4-inch strips

1 teaspoon grated gingerroot

1 clove garlic, crushed

1 medium red bell pepper, cut into 2 × 1/4-inch strips

1 cup 1/4-inch slices mushrooms (about 3 ounces)

1 cup Chinese pea pods

1 tablespoon sesame seed, toasted

Mix water, cornstarch, brown sugar, soy sauce, 2 teaspoons gingerroot and the bouillon granules; reserve. Cook and drain vermicelli as directed on package.

While vermicelli is cooking, heat wok or 12-inch nonstick skillet until 1 or 2 drops of water bubble and skitter when sprinkled in wok. Add oil; rotate wok to coat side. Add beef, 1 teaspoon gingerroot and the garlic; stir-fry about 3 minutes or until beef is brown. Add bell pepper, mushrooms and pea pods; stir-fry 1 minute.

Stir in cornstarch mixture. Cook and stir about 1 minute or until thickened. Stir in vermicelli. Sprinkle with sesame seed.

1 Serving		% Daily Value:	
Calories	270	Vitamin A	4%
Calories from fat	110	Vitamin C	26%
Fat, g	12	Calcium	2%
Saturated, g	4	Iron	20%
Cholesterol, mg	60		
Sodium, mg	420		
Carbohydrate, g	24		
Dietary Fiber, g	2		
Protein, g	19		

∾

Beef in Creamy Mushroom Sauce

6 SERVINGS

2 tablespoons cornstarch

1 cup water

1 pound lean beef boneless sirloin steak, about 1/2 inch thick

1 small onion, chopped (about 1/4 cup)

1 clove garlic, crushed

1/4 teaspoon salt

1/8 teaspoon pepper

1 medium red bell pepper, cut into bite-size pieces

3 cups sliced mushrooms (about 8 ounces)

1/4 cup brandy or water

1 teaspoon low-sodium beef bouillon granules

2 tablespoons nonfat sour cream

3 tablespoons chopped fresh chives

3 cups hot cooked mostaccioli

Stir cornstarch into water; reserve. Trim fat from beef steak. Cut beef into thin strips, about 1 1/2 × 1/2 inch. Spray 10-inch skillet with non-stick cooking spray; heat over medium-high heat. Cook onion, garlic, salt and pepper in skillet about 3 minutes, stirring frequently, until onion is tender.

Stir in beef and bell pepper. Cook about 4 minutes, stirring frequently, until beef is no longer pink. Stir in mushrooms. Add brandy to skillet; sprinkle bouillon granules over beef mixture. Heat to boiling; reduce heat. Cover and simmer 1 minute.

Stir in sour cream. Stir in cornstarch mixture. Cook over medium-high heat about 2 minutes, stirring frequently, until thickened. Stir in chives. Serve over mostaccioli.

1 Serving		% Daily Value:	
Calories	205	Vitamin A	8%
Calories from fat	25	Vitamin C	22%
Fat, g	3	Calcium	2%
Saturated, g	1	Iron	16%
Cholesterol, mg	40		
Sodium, mg	220		
Carbohydrate, g	27		
Dietary Fiber, g	2		
Protein, g	19		

Mexi Shells

6 SERVINGS

⊠ ⊻

Jumbo pasta shells are a fun change of pace, especially when stuffed with the Mexican-inspired filling here.

18 uncooked jumbo pasta shells

4 cans (8 ounces each) no-salt-added tomato sauce

2 tablespoons all-purpose flour

1 teaspoon chili powder

2 teaspoons ground cumin

3/4 pound extra-lean ground beef

1 small onion, chopped (about 1/4 cup)

1 teaspoon ground cumin

1 tablespoon chopped fresh cilantro

1 can (4 ounces) chopped green chilies, drained

1 can (15 ounces) chile beans in sauce, undrained

1 cup shredded part-skim mozzarella cheese (4 ounces)

Heat oven to 350°. Cook and drain pasta shells as directed on package. While pasta is cooking, mix tomato sauce, flour, chile powder and 2 teaspoons cumin; reserve. Cook ground beef and onion in 2-quart saucepan over medium heat, stirring occasionally, until beef is brown; drain. Stir in 1 teaspoon cumin, the cilantro, green chilies and chile beans.

Pour 1 cup of the reserved tomato sauce mixture into ungreased rectangular baking dish, 13 × 9 × 2 inches. Spoon about 1 1/2 tablespoons beef mixture into each pasta shell. Place filled sides up on sauce in dish. Pour remaining tomato sauce mixture over shells. Sprinkle with cheese. Cover and bake 30 minutes. Let stand uncovered 10 minutes before serving.

1 Serving		% Daily Value:	
Calories	300	Vitamin A	16%
Calories from fat	90	Vitamin C	20%
Fat, g	10	Calcium	14%
Saturated, g	4	Iron	24%
Cholesterol, mg	40		
Sodium, mg	550		
Carbohydrate, g	35		
Dietary Fiber, g	5		
Protein, g	22		

Pastitsio

8 SERVINGS

1 package (16 ounces) rigatoni pasta

1/2 pound extra-lean ground beef

1 medium onion, chopped (about 1/2 cup)

1/4 teaspoon salt

1/4 teaspoon ground allspice

1/4 teaspoon ground cinnamon

1/4 teaspoon ground nutmeg

1/2 cup dry white wine or water

1 can (6 ounces) no-salt-added tomato paste

1 tablespoon margarine

1/4 cup all-purpose flour

2 cans (12 ounces each) evaporated skimmed milk

1 can (14 1/2 ounces) 1/3-less-salt clear chicken broth

1/4 teaspoon pepper

1 cup crumbled feta cheese (4 ounces)

1/4 cup chopped fresh parsley

Heat oven to 350°. Grease rectangular baking dish, 13 × 9 × 2 inches. Cook and drain pasta as directed on package. While pasta is cooking, cook ground beef and onion in 10-inch nonstick skillet over medium heat, stirring occasionally, until beef is brown; drain. Stir in salt, allspice, cinnamon, nutmeg, wine and tomato paste; remove from heat and reserve.

Melt margarine in 3-quart saucepan over medium heat. Stir in flour. Cook, stirring frequently, until bubbly. Stir in milk, broth and pepper. Cook, stirring frequently with wire whisk, until mixture begins to thicken (do not boil). Stir in cheese and parsley until cheese is melted. Stir in pasta.

Spread half of the pasta mixture in baking dish. Spread beef mixture evenly over pasta mixture. Spread remaining pasta mixture over beef mixture. Bake uncovered 30 minutes.

1 Serving		% Daily Value:	
Calories	390	Vitamin A	20%
Calories from fat	90	Vitamin C	10%
Fat, g	10	Calcium	34%
Saturated, g	4	Iron	24%
Cholesterol, mg	80		
Sodium, mg	630		
Carbohydrate, g	56		
Dietary Fiber, g	4		
Protein, g	23		

Moroccan Beef with Couscous

6 SERVINGS

⬇

1 tablespoon low-sodium beef bouillon
   granules

1 cup hot water

1 pound beef boneless chuck, tip or round
   roast, cut into 1-inch cubes

2 large tomatoes, seeded and coarsely
   chopped (about 2 cups)

2 large onions, chopped (about 2 cups)

3 slices lemon, cut in half

2 cloves garlic

1/3 cup chopped fresh or 2 tablespoons
   dried cilantro leaves

1/3 cup chopped fresh Italian or regular
   parsley or 2 tablespoons dried parsley
   flakes

1 tablespoon olive or vegetable oil

1 teaspoon ground ginger

1/2 teaspoon salt

1/4 teaspoon pepper

1/8 teaspoon ground red pepper (cayenne)

1 cup uncooked couscous

1 Serving		% Daily Value:	
Calories	365	Vitamin A	6%
Calories from fat	135	Vitamin C	18%
Fat, g	15	Calcium	4%
Saturated, g	5	Iron	18%
Cholesterol, mg	60		
Sodium, mg	240		
Carbohydrate, g	35		
Dietary Fiber, g	3		
Protein, g	26		

Heat oven to 325°. Dissolve bouillon granules in hot water. Mix bouillon mixture and remaining ingredients except couscous in ungreased Dutch oven. Cover and bake 2 to 2 1/2 hours or until beef is very tender. Prepare couscous as directed on package. Serve beef mixture over couscous.

PASTA ARITHMETIC

- When preparing pasta, allow 1/2 to 3/4 cup cooked pasta per side dish or appetizer serving. If you plan to make pasta your main dish, allow 1 1/4 to 1 1/2 cups per serving.

- 1 ounce of dried pasta will yield approximately 1/2 cup of cooked pasta. This yield will vary slightly depending on the shape, type and size of pasta.

- To measure 4 ounces of spaghetti easily, make a circle with your thumb and index finger, about the size of a quarter, and fill it with pasta!

Pasta Yields

	Uncooked	Cooked	Servings
Macaroni	6 or 7 ounces	4 cups	4 to 6
Spaghetti	7 to 8 ounces	4 cups	4 to 6
Noodles	8 ounces (4 to 5 cups)	4 to 5 cups	4 to 6

Scampi with Fettuccine

4 SERVINGS

1 pound fresh or frozen raw medium shrimp (in shells)

6 ounces uncooked spinach fettuccine

2 tablespoons thinly sliced green onions

1 tablespoon chopped fresh or 1 1/2 teaspoons dried basil leaves

1 tablespoon chopped fresh parsley

2 tablespoons lemon juice

1/4 teaspoon salt

2 cloves garlic, finely chopped

Peel shrimp. (If shrimp are frozen, do not thaw; peel in cold water.) Make a shallow cut lengthwise down back of each shrimp; wash out vein. Cook and drain fettuccine as directed on package.

While fettuccine is cooking, spray 10-inch skillet with nonstick cooking spray; heat over medium heat. Add shrimp and remaining ingredients. Cook 2 to 3 minutes, stirring frequently, until shrimp are pink; remove from heat. Toss fettuccine and shrimp mixture in skillet.

1 Serving		% Daily Value:	
Calories	195	Vitamin A	4%
Calories from fat	20	Vitamin C	0%
Fat, g	2	Calcium	6%
Saturated, g	1	Iron	20%
Cholesterol, mg	145		
Sodium, mg	440		
Carbohydrate, g	29		
Dietary Fiber, g	2		
Protein, g	17		

Chilled Shrimp Fettuccine

4 SERVINGS

8 ounces uncooked fettuccine

8 ounces frozen, cooked, peeled and deveined medium shrimp, thawed and drained

1 tablespoon lemon juice

3/4 cup nonfat mayonnaise or salad dressing

1/4 cup chopped fresh parsley

1/4 cup finely chopped red onion (about 1 small)

1/4 cup nonfat Italian dressing

1 teaspoon Creole or Cajun seasoning

1/2 teaspoon freshly ground pepper

Cook and drain fettuccine as directed on package. Rinse with cold water; drain. Toss shrimp and lemon juice in large bowl. Mix remaining ingredients. Add mayonnaise mixture and fettuccine to shrimp; toss. Cover and refrigerate 1 to 2 hours to blend flavors.

1 Serving		% Daily Value:	
Calories	295	Vitamin A	6%
Calories from fat	30	Vitamin C	8%
Fat, g	3	Calcium	4%
Saturated, g	1	Iron	22%
Cholesterol, mg	130		
Sodium, mg	810		
Carbohydrate, g	54		
Dietary Fiber, g	3		
Protein, g	16		

Chilled Shrimp Fettuccine

Seafood Lasagne Roll-ups with Lemon-Caper Sauce

8 SERVINGS

8 uncooked lasagne noodles

1 tablespoon margarine

1/4 cup all-purpose flour

2 cans (12 ounces each) evaporated skimmed milk

1 tablespoon grated lemon peel

1 tablespoon chopped fresh or 1 teaspoon dried dill weed

1 1/2 tablespoons capers

1/2 cup cholesterol-free egg product

1 tablespoon chopped fresh or 1/4 teaspoon dried thyme leaves

1/2 teaspoon salt

1/2 teaspoon lemon pepper

1 small onion, finely chopped (about 1/4 cup)

8 ounces frozen, cooked, peeled and deveined medium shrimp, thawed, drained and coarsely chopped

1 container (15 ounces) nonfat ricotta cheese

1 package (10 ounces) frozen chopped broccoli, thawed and drained

1/4 teaspoon paprika

Heat oven to 350°. Cook and drain noodles as directed on package. Cover noodles with cold water. Melt margarine in 2-quart saucepan over medium heat. Mix flour and milk until smooth; pour into saucepan. Cook over medium heat, stirring occasionally until mixture begins to thicken. Stir in lemon peel, dill weed and capers. Remove from heat and reserve.

Mix 1/2 cup of the reserved sauce and the remaining ingredients except paprika. Drain noodles. Spread about 1/2 cup shrimp mixture to edges of 1 noodle. Roll up noodle. Place seam side down in greased rectangular baking dish, 13 × 9 × 2 inches. Repeat with remaining noodles. Pour remaining reserved sauce over roll-ups. Sprinkle with paprika. Bake uncovered about 30 minutes or until heated through.

1 Serving		% Daily Value:	
Calories	290	Vitamin A	26%
Calories from fat	35	Vitamin C	12%
Fat, g	4	Calcium	44%
Saturated, g	1	Iron	18%
Cholesterol, mg	65		
Sodium, mg	530		
Carbohydrate, g	41		
Dietary Fiber, g	2		
Protein, g	25		

Fresh Jamaican Jerk Tuna Salad

4 SERVINGS

⧗

1/2 pound tuna steak, 1 inch thick

2 tablespoons lemon juice

1 1/2 teaspoons chopped fresh or
  1/4 teaspoon dried thyme leaves

1 teaspoon sugar

1/2 teaspoon ground allspice

1/2 teaspoon ground red pepper (cayenne)

1/2 teaspoon freshly ground pepper

1/4 teaspoon salt

Dash of ground cloves

1 clove garlic, crushed

2 cups uncooked rotini pasta (about
  4 ounces)

2 tablespoons olive or vegetable oil

2 tablespoons tarragon vinegar

2 teaspoons chopped fresh or 1/4 teaspoon
  dried thyme leaves

1/2 teaspoon celery salt

1/4 teaspoon pepper

1 medium cucumber, coarsely chopped
  (about 1 cup)

2 tablespoons sliced green onions

4 medium tomatoes, cut into 1/2-inch slices

Set oven control to broil. Place fish steaks on rack in broiler pan. Mix lemon juice, thyme, sugar, allspice, red pepper, freshly ground pepper, salt, cloves and garlic. Brush fish with half of the lemon juice mixture. Broil with top about 4 inches from heat 7 minutes. Carefully turn fish; brush with remaining lemon juice mixture. Broil about 7 minutes longer or until fish flakes easily with fork; cool. Flake fish.

Cook and drain pasta as directed on package. Rinse with cold water; drain. Mix oil, vinegar, thyme, celery salt and pepper in large bowl. Add fish, pasta, cucumber and onions; toss. Arrange tomato slices around edge of serving platter. Spoon pasta mixture onto center of platter.

1 Serving		% Daily Value:	
Calories	275	Vitamin A	10%
Calories from fat	90	Vitamin C	24%
Fat, g	10	Calcium	4%
Saturated, g	2	Iron	16%
Cholesterol, mg	30		
Sodium, mg	370		
Carbohydrate, g	32		
Dietary Fiber, g	2		
Protein, g	16		

Pasta

Pasta used to mean just spaghetti, lasagne or noodles, but now it means so much more! From dried to fresh, short to long, curly to ridged and flat to tubular, the tremendous variety available is certainly worth exploring.

To help guide you through the multitude of enticing "pastabilities," we've identified the historical origins and names given to particular varieties.Pasta names have specific meanings representative of the shape or the intended use for preferred dishes. Despite similarity in shape, some varieties were originally referred to by different names depending on Italian regional traditions.

Pasta Glossary

Bucatini: A long, hollow noodle, thicker than spaghetti, that originated in Naples. *Bucato* literally means "with a hole." When broken into thirds and served with a sauce, this noodle will absorb the flavor inward, adding more flavor to each bite.

Capellini (Angel Hair): *Capellini,* which means "thin hair," is one of the thinnest cut spaghetti noodles. Legend has it that Parmesan cheese clings to this pasta like gold clings to angel's hair. It is a very quick pasta to prepare as it needs to boil only a few minutes and is best served with light sauces and in soups.

Couscous ("koos-koos")**:** The most tiny pasta, it is a staple of North African and some Middle Eastern cuisines. Couscous plays a dual role. It is actually granular semolina, from which pasta is made, but is most often used like rice. Couscous is available in regular and precooked varieties. Precooked couscous cooks in just five minutes.
See also Grains Glossary p. 88.

Ditalini: A pasta cut into short segments resembling thimbles. Two types are available: lisci, or smooth, which is appropriate for soups and salads, and regati, meaning grooved, which is suitable for chunky sauces. Typically it is cooked in soups or served with a vegetable sauce.

Elbow Macaroni: A short, curved, tubular-shaped pasta. This pasta is used extensively in casseroles and salads.

Farfalle (Bow ties): A bow-tie-shaped pasta. Traditionally, this pasta is accompanied by colorful sauces, reminiscent of blooming gardens, with fresh herbs or ripe vegetables such as sweet bell peppers or zucchini. Miniature bow ties are known as *tripolini* and are appropriate for soups or salads.

Fettuccine: Literally meaning "little strands," fettuccine is a long, flat noodle, usually 1/4 inch wide. Thick, smooth white sauces, such as Alfredo, cling beautifully to this pasta. Fettuccine is available in many flavors including plain and spinach.

Fusilli: A long or short curled pasta from southern Italy usually served with spicy tomato sauces. Hailing originally from Naples, it is also known as *eliche*, or "propellers," for its quality of trapping particles of the sauce and propelling them between the palate and the tongue.

Gnocchi: Any of several soft dumplings made from boiled potatoes, eggs and flour. *Gnocchi* means "lumps," due to the irregular, somewhat craggy shapes these dumplings have when cooked in soups. They range from marble to golf ball size, and are boiled and served with a butter or cream based sauce.

Lasagne: These noodles are flat and about 2 inches wide with either ruffled or straight edges. The classic Italian casserole called lasagne is made by layering cooked noodles with a red sauce and variety of cheeses and then baking. Frozen, precooked sheets (not cut) of lasagne noodles are available.

Linguine: A flat, thin noodle served with light sauces such as clam or pesto. The name means "little tongues," as its original shape resembled the thickness of a song bird's tongue.

Mafalde (Mini-Lasagne noodles): This is a long, flat, narrow noodle with curled edges, popular for sauces with seafood. Mafalde is also available in a short length and is often referred to as mini-lasagne noodles.

Manicotti (Cannelloni): A large, 4-inch tubular noodle that is usually stuffed and baked. Derived from the word canna, it means "hollow cane."

Mostaccioli: A short cut pasta about 2 inches long. These tubular "mustaches" have slanted cuts at both ends. Mostaccioli can have a smooth or grooved finish.

Penne: A short cut pasta about 1 1/4 inches long. Tubular in shape with slanted cuts at both ends, penne can have a smooth or grooved finish; it is narrower than mostaccioli. The word *penne* means "feather," indicating either the lightness of the noodle or the transversally cut shape resembling a bird's wing. It is excellent with tomato and vegetable sauces.

Continues

Radiatore: Also known as *pasta nuggets*, this pasta is shaped like car radiators. This ruffly little pasta is an excellent choice for light sauces and salads because the ruffles can catch all the flavors in the sauce or dressing.

Ravioli: Pillow-shaped pasta popular in several Italian regions, usually made with a stuffing of spinach and cheese. Ravioli are also filled with ingredients such as crabmeat or pumpkin. Traditionally served with butter or Parmesan, this pasta is also delicious with tomato and meat sauces. Due to its richness, ravioli is usually served as a main course or on special occasions.

Rigatoni: Short cut, wide tubular pasta with lengthwise grooves, about 1 inch long. It suits most chunky sauces and meat sauces.

Rosamarina (Orzo): So named for its resemblance to rice, this pasta is ideal in soups, salads and side dishes.

Rotini: A short cut pasta with a corkscrew shape that is sold plain or tricolored. A wider version of this shape is called *rotelle*. Rotini is a favorite for pasta salads.

Shells: Shells are available in jumbo, medium and small sizes. Jumbo shells are great stuffed, while medium and small shells are more suited for thick sauces, soups and salads.

Spaghetti: Means "little strings" in Italian. These long, thin strands of pasta are round and solid.

Tortelli: A round type of ravioli whose name literally means "little torte." Usually cut in a shape resembling a shining sun, it can also have a half moon shape. This pasta is usually served with light sauces so the flavor of the filling comes through.

Tortellini: Little rings of pasta filled with cheese, originally from the city of Bologna. Both plain and spinach-flavored tortellini are available; the fresh, refrigerated products are offered with a variety of fillings such as Italian sausage or chicken. Usually served with a tomato or cream sauce, tortellini is also well-suited to soups and salads. To prevent tortellini from losing its shape and filling, do not overcook it.

Vermicelli: A long, very thin pasta. "Little worms" is the original meaning of this name, which describes the squirming motion the noodles undergo when surrounded by sauce and twirled around a fork. It was the original pasta for spaghetti and meatballs. Vermicelli is well-suited for use with lighter sauces and in soups.

Ziti: A short cut, 2-inch tubular noodle with a smooth surface. It is well-suited for chunky sauces and meat sauces.

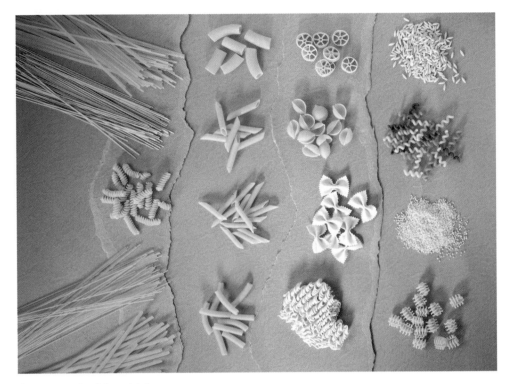

(From top, going left to right)

Row 1: Linguini, Rigatoni, Wagon Wheels, Rosamarina (Orzo)
Row 2: Buckwheat Noodles, Mostaccioli, Medium Shells, Fusilli
Row 3: Rotini, Penne, Farfalle (Bow ties), Couscous
Row 4: Vermicelli, Ziti, Asian Noodles, Radiatore
Row 5: Fettuccine

Roasted Vegetable Stew

6 SERVINGS

Roasting the vegetables adds a rich, caramelized flavor to this delicious meatless stew.

5 small red potatoes (about 12 ounces)

1 large onion, cut in half

1 medium red bell pepper, cut into fourths and seeds removed

1 medium green bell pepper, cut into fourths and seeds removed

1 medium carrot, cut into 1/4-inch diagonal slices (about 1/2 cup)

1 small zucchini, cut into 1/2-inch slices

4 ounces whole mushrooms

2 cloves garlic, chopped

2 tablespoons olive or vegetable oil

1 can (14 1/2 ounces) 1/3-less-salt clear chicken broth

2 cans (14 1/2 ounces each) Italian-style stewed tomatoes, undrained

2 cups uncooked rotini pasta (about 4 ounces)

2 tablespoons chopped fresh parsley

Set oven controls to broil. Toss potatoes, onion, bell peppers, carrot, zucchini, mushrooms, garlic and oil. Spread vegetable mixture, skin sides up, in ungreased jelly roll pan, 15 1/2 × 10 1/2 × 1 inch.

Broil with tops 4 to 6 inches from heat 15 to 20 minutes or until roasted. Remove vegetables as they become soft; cool. Remove skins from peppers. Coarsely chop vegetables.

Mix vegetables, broth and tomatoes in 3-quart saucepan. Heat to boiling over medium-high heat; reduce heat. Cover and simmer 15 minutes. Meanwhile, cook and drain pasta as directed on package. Stir pasta into vegetable mixture. Sprinkle with parsley.

1 Serving		% Daily Value:	
Calories	300	Vitamin A	38%
Calories from fat	55	Vitamin C	42%
Fat, g	6	Calcium	6%
Saturated, g	1	Iron	20%
Cholesterol, mg	10		
Sodium, mg	360		
Carbohydrate, g	58		
Dietary Fiber, g	6		
Protein, g	9		

Roasted Vegetable Stew

Minted Pesto Fusilli

6 SERVINGS

Fresh mint and cilantro replace traditional basil in this updated version of pesto.

1 package (16 ounces) fusilli pasta

1 cup nonfat cottage cheese

1/2 cup packed fresh mint leaves

1/2 cup packed fresh cilantro leaves

1/2 cup chicken broth

1 tablespoon olive or vegetable oil

2 cloves garlic, finely chopped

1 can (4 ounces) chopped green chilies, drained

2 tablespoons pine nuts, toasted

Cook and drain pasta as directed on package. While pasta is cooking, place remaining ingredients except nuts in blender or food processor. Cover and blend until smooth. Toss pasta and mint mixture. Sprinkle with nuts.

1 Serving		% Daily Value:	
Calories	345	Vitamin A	2%
Calories from fat	45	Vitamin C	22%
Fat, g	5	Calcium	2%
Saturated, g	1	Iron	18%
Cholesterol, mg	2		
Sodium, mg	590		
Carbohydrate, g	63		
Dietary Fiber, g	3		
Protein, g	15		

Broccoli and Artichoke Pasta

4 SERVINGS

This contemporary side dish has bold flavor that goes very nicely with grilled beef.

4 ounces uncooked spaghetti

1 jar (6 ounces) marinated artichoke hearts, drained and marinade reserved

2 cups broccoli flowerets

1/4 cup crumbled feta cheese (2 ounces)

**2 tablespoons chopped fresh or
3/4 teaspoon dried oregano leaves**

1 tablespoon lemon juice

Cook and drain spaghetti as directed on package. Rinse with cold water; drain. Coarsely chop artichoke hearts. Toss spaghetti, artichoke hearts, reserved marinade and remaining ingredients. Cover and refrigerate 1 to 2 hours to blend flavors.

1 Serving		% Daily Value:	
Calories	190	Vitamin A	8%
Calories from fat	45	Vitamin C	38%
Fat, g	5	Calcium	12%
Saturated, g	3	Iron	12%
Cholesterol, mg	15		
Sodium, mg	410		
Carbohydrate, g	31		
Dietary Fiber, g	3		
Protein, g	8		

Broccoli and Artichoke Pasta, Italian Bean Soup (page 53)

Spaghetti Torte

8 SERVINGS

For a new twist on spaghetti, try this simple torte. It cuts and serves easily, too!

1 package (16 ounces) spaghetti

1/2 cup reduced-fat grated Parmesan-style cheese (2 ounces)

1/2 cup light ricotta cheese

1 tablespoon Italian seasoning

1/2 cup cholesterol-free egg product

1/4 cup finely chopped fresh or 1 1/2 teaspoons dried basil leaves

2 medium tomatoes, each cut into 5 slices

4 slices (1 ounce each) provolone cheese, cut in half

Heat oven to 350°. Spray springform pan, 9 × 3 inches, with nonstick cooking spray. Cook and drain spaghetti as directed on package. Rinse with cold water; drain. Toss spaghetti, Parmesan cheese, ricotta cheese, Italian seasoning and egg product until spaghetti is well coated.

Press half the spaghetti mixture in bottom of pan. Sprinkle with half of the basil. Layer with half the tomato and cheese slices. Press remaining spaghetti mixture on top. Sprinkle with remaining basil. Layer with remaining tomato and cheese slices. Bake 30 minutes. Let stand 15 minutes. Remove side of pan. Cut torte into wedges to serve.

1 Serving		% Daily Value:	
Calories	335	Vitamin A	10%
Calories from fat	80	Vitamin C	4%
Fat, g	9	Calcium	28%
Saturated, g	5	Iron	16%
Cholesterol, mg	25		
Sodium, mg	550		
Carbohydrate, g	49		
Dietary Fiber, g	2		
Protein, g	17		

Garden-fresh Primavera

4 SERVINGS

Bottled Italian salad dressing provides zesty flavor in this easy main dish.

8 ounces uncooked linguine

1 cup 1-inch pieces green beans (about 4 ounces)

1 cup 1/4-inch slices mushrooms (about 3 ounces)

1 medium tomato, cut into 1-inch pieces

1 medium carrot, cut into 1/4-inch diagonal slices (about 1/2 cup)

1/2 medium green bell pepper, cut into 2 × 1/4-inch pieces

1 bottle (8 ounces) nonfat Italian dressing

Freshly cracked pepper, if desired

Cook linguine as directed on package, adding green beans during last 1 minute of cooking. Drain linguine and beans. Rinse with cold water; drain.

Toss linguine, beans and remaining ingredients except pepper. Cover and refrigerate 1 to 2 hours to blend flavors. Serve with pepper.

1 Serving		% Daily Value:	
Calories	240	Vitamin A	32%
Calories from fat	10	Vitamin C	30%
Fat, g	1	Calcium	2%
Saturated, g	0	Iron	16%
Cholesterol, mg	0		
Sodium, mg	690		
Carbohydrate, g	54		
Dietary Fiber, g	6		
Protein, g	9		

Vegetable Lasagne

8 SERVINGS

▼

When sliced, this lasagne reveals pretty layers of white, red, yellow and green.

9 uncooked lasagne noodles

1 container (15 ounces) nonfat ricotta cheese

1 package (10 ounces) frozen chopped spinach, thawed and squeezed to drain

1/2 teaspoon salt

1/2 teaspoon fennel seed

1/2 cup cholesterol-free egg product

Easy Homemade Tomato Sauce (page 71) or 4 1/2 cups purchased spaghetti sauce

2 medium zucchini, cut into 1/4-inch slices (about 2 cups)

1 medium yellow summer squash, cut into 1/4-inch slices (about 2 cups)

3 cups shredded part-skim mozzarella cheese (12 ounces)

Heat oven to 350°. Cook and drain noodles as directed on package. Mix ricotta cheese, spinach, salt, fennel seed and egg product.

Spread 1/2 cup of the Easy Homemade Tomato Sauce in bottom of ungreased rectangular baking dish, 13 × 9 × 2 inches. Layer with 3 noodles, 1 cup of the spaghetti sauce, half the spinach mixture, half the zucchini, half the squash and 1 cup of the mozzarella cheese; repeat. Top with remaining 3 noodles, sauce and mozzarella cheese. Bake uncovered 25 to 30 minutes or until hot and bubbly. Let stand 15 minutes before cutting.

1 Serving		% Daily Value:	
Calories	405	Vitamin A	40%
Calories from fat	135	Vitamin C	12%
Fat, g	15	Calcium	56%
Saturated, g	6	Iron	20%
Cholesterol, mg	35		
Sodium, mg	1520		
Carbohydrate, g	45		
Dietary Fiber, g	4		
Protein, g	26		

Parmesan-Peppercorn Linguine

4 SERVINGS

12 ounces uncooked linguine

1 teaspoon margarine

1 clove garlic, crushed

2 tablespoons all-purpose flour

1 teaspoon black peppercorns, crushed

1/2 teaspoon freshly ground pepper

2 cups skim milk

1/4 cup freshly grated Parmesan cheese (1 ounce)

Cook and drain linguine as directed on package. While linguine is cooking, melt margarine in 12-inch skillet over medium heat. Cook garlic in margarine, stirring occasionally, until garlic is golden brown. Stir in flour, peppercorns, pepper and milk. Heat to boiling, stirring frequently with wire whisk. Boil and stir 1 minute; remove from heat. Stir in cheese. Toss linguine and sauce.

1 Serving		% Daily Value:	
Calories	415	Vitamin A	8%
Calories from fat	45	Vitamin C	2%
Fat, g	5	Calcium	26%
Saturated, g	2	Iron	22%
Cholesterol, mg	10		
Sodium, mg	530		
Carbohydrate, g	78		
Dietary Fiber, g	3		
Protein, g	18		

Olive Lover's Pasta

4 SERVINGS

4 cups uncooked rotini pasta (about 8 ounces)

2 tablespoons olive or vegetable oil

3 tablespoons red wine vinegar

2 tablespoons chopped fresh or 1 1/2 teaspoons dried oregano leaves

1/4 teaspoon salt

1/4 to 1/2 teaspoon crushed red pepper

2 cloves garlic, crushed

2 tablespoons sliced pimiento-stuffed olives

2 tablespoons sliced ripe olives

2 cups broccoli flowerets

2 medium zucchini, cut into 1/4-inch slices (about 2 cups)

Cook and drain pasta as directed on package. While pasta is cooking, heat oil, vinegar, oregano, salt, red pepper and garlic in 10-inch nonstick skillet. Cook olives, broccoli and zucchini in oil mixture, stirring occasionally, until broccoli is crisp-tender. Serve over pasta.

1 Serving		% Daily Value:	
Calories	300	Vitamin A	22%
Calories from fat	90	Vitamin C	34%
Fat, g	10	Calcium	12%
Saturated, g	2	Iron	24%
Cholesterol, mg	0		
Sodium, mg	550		
Carbohydrate, g	48		
Dietary Fiber, g	7		
Protein, g	11		

Chicken Chow Mein Soup

6 SERVINGS

2 cups cubed cooked chicken (about 12 ounces)

2 medium stalks celery, sliced (about 1 cup)

1 cup 1/4-inch slices mushrooms (about 3 ounces)

1 cup bean sprouts

1 cup shredded green cabbage

1/4 cup shredded carrot

1/4 cup sliced green onions (2 to 3 medium)

2 3/4 cups water

1/4 cup dry sherry or water

3 tablespoons low-sodium soy sauce

4 ounces uncooked vermicelli, broken into thirds

1 can (14 1/2 ounces) 1/3-less-salt clear chicken broth

1 can (8 ounces) sliced bamboo shoots, drained

Heat all ingredients to boiling in 3-quart saucepan over medium-high heat, stirring occasionally; reduce heat. Cover and simmer 10 minutes.

1 Serving		% Daily Value:	
Calories	200	Vitamin A	16%
Calories from fat	35	Vitamin C	6%
Fat, g	4	Calcium	4%
Saturated, g	1	Iron	16%
Cholesterol, mg	35		
Sodium, mg	380		
Carbohydrate, g	23		
Dietary Fiber, g	3		
Protein, g	21		

Italian Bean Soup

6 SERVINGS

1 teaspoon vegetable oil

1 medium onion, chopped (about 1/2 cup)

1 clove garlic, crushed

1 1/2 cups chopped fully cooked smoked reduced-sodium ham (about 3/4 pound)

1 cup uncooked elbow macaroni (about 4 ounces)

1/2 teaspoon Italian seasoning

1/8 teaspoon red pepper sauce

3 roma (plum) tomatoes, seeded and chopped (about 1 cup)

1 medium stalk celery, cut into 1/4-inch diagonal slices (about 1/2 cup)

2 cans (14 1/2 ounces each) 1/3-less-salt clear chicken broth

1 can (15 to 16 ounces) great northern beans, rinsed and drained

Heat oil in 3-quart saucepan over medium-high heat. Cook onion and garlic in oil, stirring frequently, until onion is tender. Stir in remaining ingredients. Heat to boiling; reduce heat. Cover and simmer 12 to 15 minutes or until macaroni is tender.

1 Serving		% Daily Value:	
Calories	225	Vitamin A	2%
Calories from fat	35	Vitamin C	12%
Fat, g	4	Calcium	6%
Saturated, g	1	Iron	22%
Cholesterol, mg	20		
Sodium, mg	450		
Carbohydrate, g	35		
Dietary Fiber, g	4		
Protein, g	16		

Selection, Storage and Cooking
Pasta Primer

Selection

Pasta is available in three forms: dried, fresh and frozen. Dried pasta is usually found prepackaged or in self-serve bulk form. Fresh pasta can be found in the refrigerated section of the supermarket. The most common varieties of frozen pasta are lasagne noodles, egg noodles and filled tortellini or ravioli.

- When purchasing dried pasta, look for smooth, unbroken pasta.

- Avoid dried pasta with a marblelike (many fine lines) surface; this indicates a problem with the way it dried and it may fall apart during cooking.

- When purchasing fresh pasta, look for smooth, unbroken pasta with consistent color throughout the shape. Although fresh pasta should appear dry, it shouldn't appear brittle or crumbly. Avoid packages containing moisture droplets or liquid, which could indicate molding or mushy pasta.

- When purchasing frozen pasta, avoid packages containing ice crystals or those in which the pasta pieces are frozen together in a solid mass. Avoid pasta that is freezer burned (dry, white spots).

Storage

Uncooked Dried Pasta: Most dried pasta can be stored indefinitely, but for optimum quality and flavor, a 1- to 2-year storage time is recommended.

- Store in original packaging or transfer to airtight glass or plastic containers and label contents with starting storage date.

- Store in a cool (60° or less), dry location.

Uncooked Fresh Pasta: Fresh pasta is perishable and should be stored in the refrigerator. Most fresh pasta packages carry use-by or expiration dates.

- Store unopened pasta in original packaging.

- Cover opened, unused portions of pasta tightly to avoid drying.

Uncooked Frozen Pasta: Frozen pasta should be stored in the freezer until ready to cook.

- Store unopened pasta in original packaging.

- Store opened, unused portions tightly sealed to avoid freezer burn and drying.

- Freeze unopened pasta for up to 9 months.

- Freeze opened pasta for up to 3 months.

Cooked Dried, Fresh and Frozen Pasta: To prevent sticking, cooked pasta can be tossed with a small amount of oil. Store in tightly sealed containers or plastic bags in the refrigerator for up to 5 days.

Cooking

Always cook pasta uncovered at a fast and continuous boil, using plenty of water. This allows the pasta to move freely, promoting even cooking. Be sure the water is boiling before adding pasta.

- Do not add oil to the cooking water; sauces will not cling to oil-coated pasta.

- Salting the cooking water is optional and not necessary for the proper cooking of pasta.

- Use at least 1 quart water (4 cups) for every 4 ounces of pasta.

- Follow package directions for cooking times. Fresh pasta cooks faster than dried pasta. Cooked pasta should be tender but firm to the bite (*al dente*).

- Stir pasta frequently to prevent sticking.

- Do not rinse pasta after draining unless stated in the recipe. Pasta is usually rinsed when it is to be used in salads.

THE PERFECT MATCH

～∾～

The perfect pairing of pasta and sauce can greatly enhance both the flavor of the dish as well as the ease of eating the dish. Some shapes can be used in several different ways. Use the simple guidelines below for the perfect match.

Flat, Narrow and Thin Shapes (capellini, fettuccine, linguine, spaghetti, vermicelli): Smoother, thinner sauces or those with very finely chopped ingredients are the best choice because they will cling better to the large surface area of these pastas. Examples include: Alfredo Sauce (p. 71), Easy Homemade Tomato Sauce (p. 71), Gorgonzola Linguine with Toasted Walnuts (p. 58).

Short, Wide and Sturdy Shapes (mostaccioli, penne, rotelle, rotini, ziti): Chunky or heavy sauces are the best choice because the pasta is strong enough to hold up to these ingredients. Examples include: Caribbean Sausage and Peppers (p. 31), Fresh Jamaican Jerk Tuna Salad (p. 41), Onion-smothered Pasta (p. 68), Olive Lover's Pasta (p. 52)

Hollow Shapes, Twist Shapes and Shapes with Crevices (radiatore, rigatoni, rotelle, rotini, shells): Sauces with small pieces of meat and vegetables are a good choice because the pasta can capture these bits in their crevices and hollow areas. Examples include: Golden Nuggets (p. 69), Roasted Vegetable Stew (p. 46), Mexi Shells (p. 35), Salsa Pasta (p. 68), Pastitso (p. 36)

Fresh Mushroom Fettuccine

8 SERVINGS

▣

This fettucine is wonderful with any combination of fresh mushrooms—combine your favorites for a personalized dish.

8 ounces uncooked fettuccine

3 cups sliced mushrooms (about 8 ounces)

1/4 cup chopped fresh parsley

1/4 cup red wine vinegar

1/4 cup olive or vegetable oil

3 tablespoons freshly grated Parmesan cheese

2 teaspoons chopped fresh rosemary leaves

1/2 teaspoon freshly ground pepper

1/4 teaspoon salt

1 clove garlic, crushed

Cook and drain fettuccine as directed on package. Rinse with cold water; drain. Toss fettuccine and remaining ingredients.

1 Serving		% Daily Value:	
Calories	175	Vitamin A	2%
Calories from fat	80	Vitamin C	2%
Fat, g	9	Calcium	4%
Saturated, g	2	Iron	10%
Cholesterol, mg	25		
Sodium, mg	230		
Carbohydrate, g	21		
Dietary Fiber, g	2		
Protein, g	5		

Gorgonzola Linguine with Toasted Walnuts

6 SERVINGS

4 ounces uncooked linguine

1 tablespoon margarine

1 clove garlic, crushed

1 tablespoon all-purpose flour

1 cup evaporated skimmed milk

1/4 cup dry white wine or chicken broth

1/4 teaspoon salt

1/2 cup crumbled Gorgonzola cheese (about 2 ounces)

2 tablespoons walnuts, toasted and finely chopped

Cook and drain linguine as directed on package. While linguine is cooking, melt margarine in 2-quart saucepan over medium heat. Cook garlic in margarine, stirring occasionally, until garlic is golden brown. Stir in flour until smooth and bubbly. Stir in milk, wine and salt. Cook, stirring occasionally, until mixture begins to thicken.

Reduce heat to medium-low. Stir cheese into sauce. Cook, stirring occasionally, until cheese is melted. Toss linguine and sauce. Sprinkle with walnuts.

1 Serving		% Daily Value:	
Calories	185	Vitamin A	10%
Calories from fat	65	Vitamin C	0%
Fat, g	7	Calcium	18%
Saturated, g	2	Iron	6%
Cholesterol, mg	10		
Sodium, mg	370		
Carbohydrate, g	22		
Dietary Fiber, g	0		
Protein, g	8		

Greek Couscous Salad

7 SERVINGS

10 sun-dried tomato halves (not oil-packed)

1 1/2 cups cold cooked couscous

1 small unpeeled cucumber, seeded and coarsely chopped (about 3/4 cup)

2 tablespoons chopped fresh parsley or 2 teaspoons dried parsley flakes

1 tablespoon chopped fresh or 1 teaspoon dried basil leaves

2 ounces feta cheese, crumbled (about 1/3 cup)

1 tablespoon pine nuts, toasted

1 tablespoon olive or vegetable oil

1 tablespoon lemon juice

1 1/2 teaspoons chopped fresh or 1/2 teaspoon dried oregano leaves

1/4 teaspoon salt

1/8 teaspoon coarsely ground pepper

Pour enough hot water over sun-dried tomatoes to cover. Let stand 10 to 15 minutes or until softened; drain and coarsely chop.

Mix tomatoes, couscous, cucumber, parsley, basil, cheese and nuts in large bowl. Mix remaining ingredients. Pour over couscous mixture; toss. Cover and refrigerate 1 to 2 hours to blend flavors.

1 Serving		% Daily Value:	
Calories	105	Vitamin A	6%
Calories from fat	45	Vitamin C	26%
Fat, g	5	Calcium	4%
Saturated, g	2	Iron	4%
Cholesterol, mg	5		
Sodium, mg	260		
Carbohydrate, g	13		
Dietary Fiber, g	1		
Protein, g	3		

Greek Couscous Salad

Gingered Tomato and Jicama with Linguine

6 SERVINGS

4 ounces uncooked linguine

8 roma (plum) tomatoes, seeded

1 cup 1 × 1/2 × 1/4-inch strips jicama

1 tablespoon sliced green onion

1 teaspoon grated lime peel

1 tablespoon lime juice

2 teaspoons grated gingerroot

1/4 teaspoon salt

Cook and drain linguine as directed on package. Rinse with cold water; drain. Toss remaining ingredients. Serve over linguine.

1 Serving		% Daily Value:	
Calories	110	Vitamin A	8%
Calories from fat	10	Vitamin C	24%
Fat, g	1	Calcium	2%
Saturated, g	0	Iron	8%
Cholesterol, mg	0		
Sodium, mg	180		
Carbohydrate, g	24		
Dietary Fiber, g	3		
Protein, g	4		

Nutty Pasta

6 SERVINGS

The sophisticated combination of cardamom, cilantro, papaya and chopped peanuts adds excitement to this exotic side dish.

4 ounces uncooked vermicelli

2 tablespoons chopped fresh cilantro

1 tablespoon peanut oil

1/2 teaspoon salt

1/2 teaspoon ground cardamom

1 medium red bell pepper, cut into 2 × 1/4-inch strips

1 papaya or large peach, chopped (about 1 cup)

1 medium tomato, chopped (about 3/4 cup)

1/4 cup cocktail peanuts, chopped

Cook and drain vermicelli as directed on package. Rinse with cold water; drain. Toss vermicelli and remaining ingredients except peanuts. Sprinkle with peanuts.

1 Serving		% Daily Value:	
Calories	135	Vitamin A	10%
Calories from fat	45	Vitamin C	40%
Fat, g	5	Calcium	2%
Saturated, g	1	Iron	2%
Cholesterol, mg	0		
Sodium, mg	280		
Carbohydrate, g	21		
Dietary Fiber, g	2		
Protein, g	4		

Orzo with Mushrooms and Chives

4 SERVINGS

1 tablespoon margarine

1 cup uncooked rosamarina (orzo) pasta (about 6 ounces)

1 cup 1/4-inch slices mushrooms (about 3 ounces)

2 tablespoons chopped fresh chives

1 teaspoon chopped fresh or 1/8 teaspoon dried thyme leaves

1 can (14 1/2 ounces) 1/3-less-salt clear chicken broth

2 tablespoons cold water

1 teaspoon cornstarch

Melt margarine in 2-quart saucepan over medium heat. Cook pasta in margarine 3 to 4 minutes, stirring occasionally, until pasta is golden brown. Stir in mushrooms, chives, thyme and broth. Heat to boiling. Boil 10 minutes, stirring occasionally. Mix water and cornstarch; stir into pasta mixture. Cook 1 minute.

1 Serving		% Daily Value:	
Calories	165	Vitamin A	4%
Calories from fat	35	Vitamin C	0%
Fat, g	4	Calcium	2%
Saturated, g	1	Iron	12%
Cholesterol, mg	0		
Sodium, mg	60		
Carbohydrate, g	28		
Dietary Fiber, g	2		
Protein, g	6		

Three-Pepper Pasta

6 SERVINGS

3 cups uncooked farfalle (bow tie) pasta (about 8 ounces)

1 tablespoon olive or vegetable oil

1 small green bell pepper, cut into 1/4-inch strips

1 small red bell pepper, cut into 1/4-inch strips

1 small yellow bell pepper, cut into 1/4-inch strips

1 cup Easy Homemade Tomato Sauce (page 71) or purchased spaghetti sauce

Cook and drain pasta as directed on package. While pasta is cooking, heat oil in 10-inch non-stick skillet over medium heat. Cook bell peppers in oil about 5 minutes, stirring occasionally, until crisp-tender. Stir in Easy Homemade Tomato Sauce. Cook until heated through. Serve over pasta. Serve with chopped fresh basil and Parmesan cheese, if desired.

1 Serving		% Daily Value:	
Calories	105	Vitamin A	8%
Calories from fat	25	Vitamin C	32%
Fat, g	3	Calcium	2%
Saturated, g	0	Iron	6%
Cholesterol, mg	0		
Sodium, mg	200		
Carbohydrate, g	18		
Dietary Fiber, g	2		
Protein, g	3		

Three-Pepper Pasta

Minted Melon and Pasta Salad

6 SERVINGS

3 cups uncooked farfalle (bow tie) pasta (about 8 ounces)

1 container (8 ounces) orange or lemon nonfat yogurt

2 tablespoons orange juice

1 cantaloupe, cubed (about 3 1/2 cups)

2 ounces prosciutto or fully cooked smoked ham, cut into 1/2-inch strips (about 1/2 cup)

2 teaspoons chopped fresh or 1/4 teaspoon dried mint leaves

Cook and drain pasta as directed on package. Rinse with cold water; drain. Mix yogurt and orange juice in large bowl. Add pasta and remaining ingredients; toss. Cover and refrigerate 1 to 2 hours to blend flavors.

1 Serving		% Daily Value:	
Calories	205	Vitamin A	28%
Calories from fat	25	Vitamin C	34%
Fat, g	3	Calcium	6%
Saturated, g	1	Iron	12%
Cholesterol, mg	40		
Sodium, mg	280		
Carbohydrate, g	38		
Dietary Fiber, g	2		
Protein, g	9		

Turkey-Macaroni Salad

6 SERVINGS

1 1/2 cups uncooked elbow macaroni (about 6 ounces)

1 package (10 ounces) frozen green peas

2 cups cut-up cooked turkey

3/4 cup nonfat mayonnaise or salad dressing

1/2 cup shredded reduced-fat Cheddar cheese (2 ounces)

1/2 cup sliced green onions (about 5 medium)

1/4 cup sweet pickle relish

1 medium stalk celery, sliced (about 1/2 cup)

3 cups bite-size pieces lettuce (about 1/2 medium head)

Cook and drain macaroni as directed on package. Rinse with cold water; drain. Rinse frozen peas with cold water to separate; drain. Mix macaroni, peas and remaining ingredients except lettuce. Cover and refrigerate 2 to 4 hours to blend flavors. Serve on lettuce.

1 Serving		% Daily Value:	
Calories	280	Vitamin A	6%
Calories from fat	45	Vitamin C	14%
Fat, g	5	Calcium	10%
Saturated, g	2	Iron	16%
Cholesterol, mg	45		
Sodium, mg	710		
Carbohydrate, g	40		
Dietary Fiber, g	4		
Protein, g	23		

Turkey-Macaroni Salad

Antipasto Pasta

6 SERVINGS

⧗ ⩔

This beautiful cold salad is based on the classic Italian appetizer antipasto.

3 cups uncooked farfalle (bow-tie) pasta (about 8 ounces)

1/4 cup red wine vinegar

1 tablespoon finely chopped fresh or 1 teaspoon dried basil leaves

1 tablespoon capers

2 tablespoons olive or vegetable oil

1/4 teaspoon garlic powder

1/2 cup cubed part-skim mozzarella cheese (2 ounces)

1/2 cup chopped drained pepperoncini peppers

1/4 cup ripe olives, halved

1/4 cup (1 ounce) sliced pepperoni (about 20 slices)

1 medium red bell pepper, cut into 2 × 1/4-inch strips

1/2 medium zucchini, cut lengthwise in half, then crosswise into 1/4-inch slices (about 1/2 cup)

1 package (9 ounces) frozen artichoke hearts, thawed and quartered

Cook and drain pasta as directed on package. Rinse with cold water; drain. Mix vinegar, basil, capers, oil and garlic powder. Toss pasta, vinegar mixture and remaining ingredients. Cover and refrigerate about 1 hour or until chilled.

1 Serving		% Daily Value:	
Calories	260	Vitamin A	10%
Calories from fat	100	Vitamin C	30%
Fat, g	11	Calcium	12%
Saturated, g	3	Iron	14%
Cholesterol, mg	45		
Sodium, mg	410		
Carbohydrate, g	33		
Dietary Fiber, g	4		
Protein, g	11		

Antipasto Pasta

Salsa Pasta

6 SERVINGS

With only 5 ingredients, this is an easy side dish for any night of the week!

1 package (7 ounces) elbow macaroni (2 cups)

1 cup frozen whole kernel corn

1 cup salsa

1 small green bell pepper, chopped (about 1/2 cup)

1 can (14 1/2 ounces) no-salt-added whole tomatoes, undrained

Cook and drain macaroni as directed on package. While macaroni is cooking, heat remaining ingredients to boiling in 2-quart saucepan over medium heat, breaking up tomatoes. Reduce heat to low. Simmer uncovered 5 minutes. Stir in macaroni. Serve with freshly ground pepper if desired.

1 Serving		% Daily Value:	
Calories	175	Vitamin A	8%
Calories from fat	10	Vitamin C	16%
Fat, g	1	Calcium	2%
Saturated, g	0	Iron	12%
Cholesterol, mg	0		
Sodium, mg	560		
Carbohydrate, g	38		
Dietary Fiber, g	3		
Protein, g	6		

Onion-smothered Pasta

6 SERVINGS

3 cups uncooked ziti pasta (about 8 ounces)

1 tablespoon olive or vegetable oil

4 medium onions, cut into 1/4-inch slices (about 4 cups)

1/2 cup water

1/4 cup dry red wine or beef broth

1 tablespoon chopped fresh or 1 teaspoon dried basil leaves

1 tablespoon chopped fresh or 1 teaspoon dried oregano leaves

1 can (8 ounces) no-salt-added tomato sauce

Cook and drain pasta as directed on package. While pasta is cooking, heat oil in 3-quart non-stick saucepan over medium heat. Cook onions in oil 8 to 10 minutes, stirring occasionally, until tender. Stir in remaining ingredients; heat through. Serve over pasta. Sprinkle with additional oregano if desired.

1 Serving		% Daily Value:	
Calories	210	Vitamin A	4%
Calories from fat	35	Vitamin C	10%
Fat, g	4	Calcium	6%
Saturated, g	1	Iron	14%
Cholesterol, mg	0		
Sodium, mg	120		
Carbohydrate, g	42		
Dietary Fiber, g	5		
Protein, g	7		

Sichuan Pasta Toss

8 SERVINGS

3 1/2 cups uncooked Chinese egg noodles
(about 6 ounces)

1 package (16 ounces) frozen broccoli,
cauliflower, carrots and red pepper,
thawed and drained

1 can (8 ounces) sliced water chestnuts,
drained

1 jar (7 ounces) whole baby corn, drained
Sichuan Dressing (below)

Cook and drain noodles as directed on package. Toss noodles, vegetables and remaining ingredients. Cover and refrigerate 1 to 2 hours to blend flavors, stirring twice.

Sichuan Dressing

2 tablespoons vegetable oil

2 tablespoons low-sodium soy sauce

2 tablespoons dry sherry or water

2 tablespoons rice wine or balsamic or wine
vinegar

2 teaspoons sugar

1 teaspoon sesame oil

1 teaspoon chile oil or 1/4 teaspoon ground
red pepper (cayenne)

1/4 teaspoon salt

Shake all ingredients in tightly covered container.

1 Serving		% Daily Value:	
Calories	130	Vitamin A	38%
Calories from fat	35	Vitamin C	16%
Fat, g	4	Calcium	2%
Saturated, g	1	Iron	6%
Cholesterol, mg	0		
Sodium, mg	370		
Carbohydrate, g	24		
Dietary Fiber, g	3		
Protein, g	3		

Golden Nuggets

6 SERVINGS

Delightfully refreshing, this pretty pasta dish is terrific with grilled chicken.

4 sun-dried tomato halves (not oil-packed)

3 cups uncooked radiatore (nugget) pasta
(about 8 ounces)

1/4 cup freshly grated Parmesan cheese
(1 ounce)

1/4 cup chopped fresh or 1 1/2 teaspoons
dried basil leaves

3 tablespoons grated lemon peel

2 tablespoons olive or vegetable oil

2 tablespoons lemon juice

1/4 teaspoon salt

Pour enough hot water over sun-dried tomatoes to cover. Let stand 10 to 15 minutes or until softened; drain and chop. Cook and drain pasta as directed on package. Rinse with cold water; drain.

Toss pasta, tomatoes and remaining ingredients. Cover and refrigerate 1 to 2 hours to blend flavors.

1 Serving		% Daily Value:	
Calories	195	Vitamin A	4%
Calories from fat	65	Vitamin C	10%
Fat, g	7	Calcium	8%
Saturated, g	2	Iron	10%
Cholesterol, mg	35		
Sodium, mg	340		
Carbohydrate, g	28		
Dietary Fiber, g	2		
Protein, g	7		

Roasted Red Pepper Mostaccioli

6 SERVINGS

3 cups uncooked mostaccioli pasta (about 8 ounces)

1 can (14 1/2 ounces) Italian-style stewed tomatoes, undrained

1 jar (7 ounces) roasted red bell peppers, drained

1 teaspoon olive or vegetable oil

1 clove garlic, crushed

2 teaspoons finely chopped fresh or 1/2 teaspoon dried oregano leaves

2 teaspoons capers

Cook and drain pasta as directed on package. While pasta is cooking, place tomatoes and peppers in blender or food processor. Cover and blend until smooth. Heat oil in 1-quart nonstick saucepan over medium heat. Cook garlic in oil, stirring occasionally, until garlic is golden brown. Stir in tomato mixture, oregano and capers. Simmer uncovered 15 minutes, stirring occasionally. Serve over pasta. Serve with freshly ground pepper if desired.

1 Serving		% Daily Value:	
Calories	185	Vitamin A	16%
Calories from fat	35	Vitamin C	50%
Fat, g	4	Calcium	2%
Saturated, g	1	Iron	12%
Cholesterol, mg	0		
Sodium, mg	340		
Carbohydrate, g	34		
Dietary Fiber, g	3		
Protein, g	6		

Italian Stuffed Tomatoes

6 SERVINGS

4 sun-dried tomato halves (not oil-packed)

6 large tomatoes

1 cup uncooked rosamarina (orzo) pasta (6 ounces)

1/2 cup nonfat ricotta cheese

2 tablespoons pine nuts, toasted

1 tablespoon chopped fresh or 1 teaspoon dried oregano leaves

1/4 teaspoon salt

1 clove garlic, crushed

1/2 cup water

Heat oven to 350°. Pour enough hot water over sun-dried tomatoes to cover. Let stand 10 to 15 minutes or until softened; drain and chop. Cut tops off fresh tomatoes; remove and discard centers, using spoon, leaving 1/4-inch walls. Reserve tomato shells.

Cook and drain pasta as directed on package. Rinse with cold water; drain. Mix pasta, chopped sun-dried tomatoes and remaining ingredients except water. Spoon about 1/3 cup pasta mixture into each tomato shell. Place tomatoes, filled sides up, in ungreased rectangular baking dish, 13 × 9 × 2 inches. Pour water into dish. Bake uncovered 20 minutes.

1 Serving		% Daily Value:	
Calories	185	Vitamin A	14%
Calories from fat	25	Vitamin C	34%
Fat, g	3	Calcium	8%
Saturated, g	1	Iron	12%
Cholesterol, mg	2		
Sodium, mg	250		
Carbohydrate, g	34		
Dietary Fiber, g	3		
Protein, g	8		

Easy Homemade Tomato Sauce

ABOUT **4 1/2** CUPS SAUCE

1 tablespoon olive or vegetable oil

4 cloves garlic, finely chopped

1 small onion, chopped (about 1/4 cup)

2 cans (28 ounces each) whole Italian-style tomatoes, drained

2 tablespoons chopped fresh or 1 teaspoon dried basil leaves

2 teaspoons chopped fresh or 1/2 teaspoon dried oregano leaves

1/2 teaspoon salt

1/2 teaspoon pepper

Heat oil in 3-quart saucepan over medium-high heat. Cook garlic and onion in oil, stirring frequently, until onion is tender. Place tomatoes in food processor or blender. Cover and process until smooth.

Stir tomatoes and remaining ingredients into onion mixture. Heat to boiling; reduce heat. Simmer uncovered 45 minutes, stirring occasionally.

1 Serving (1/2 cup)		% Daily Value:	
Calories	45	Vitamin A	8%
Calories from fat	20	Vitamin C	16%
Fat, g	2	Calcium	4%
Saturated, g	0	Iron	4%
Cholesterol, mg	0		
Sodium, mg	330		
Carbohydrate, g	7		
Dietary Fiber, g	1		
Protein, g	1		

Alfredo Sauce

1 1/2 CUPS SAUCE

2 tablespoons margarine

1 1/2 cups evaporated skimmed milk

1 tablespoon flour

1/4 teaspoon salt

1/8 teaspoon pepper

2 tablespoons freshly grated Parmesan cheese

1/2 teaspoon freshly grated nutmeg

Melt margarine in 3-quart saucepan over medium-high heat. Mix milk, flour, salt and pepper until smooth; pour into saucepan. Heat to boiling. Boil 1 minute, stirring frequently with wire whisk; remove from heat. Stir in cheese and nutmeg.

1 Serving (1/4 cup)		% Daily Value:	
Calories	90	Vitamin A	12%
Calories from fat	35	Vitamin C	0%
Fat, g	4	Calcium	20%
Saturated, g	1	Iron	0%
Cholesterol, mg	5		
Sodium, mg	240		
Carbohydrate, g	7		
Dietary Fiber, g	1		
Protein, g	1		

2

Great Grains

⌇∽

Wild Rice–Turkey Salad with Raspberry Vinaigrette (page 114)

Jambalaya

4 SERVINGS

2 teaspoons vegetable oil

1/2 pound skinless, boneless chicken thighs, cut into 3/4-inch cubes

1/2 pound fully cooked reduced-fat turkey kielbasa sausage, cut into 1/4-inch slices

1 medium onion, sliced (about 1 cup)

1 medium green bell pepper, coarsely chopped (about 1 cup)

1 medium stalk celery, sliced (about 1/2 cup)

1 cup water

1 tablespoon all-purpose flour

1 can (14 1/2 ounces) no-salt-added whole tomatoes, undrained

2 tablespoons steak sauce

1/4 to 1/2 teaspoon red pepper sauce

2 cups cooked brown or white rice

Heat oil in nonstick Dutch oven over medium heat. Cook chicken in oil 8 to 10 minutes, stirring occasionally, until light brown. Stir in sausage, onion, bell pepper and celery. Cook, stirring frequently, until vegetables are crisp-tender.

Mix water and flour; stir into chicken mixture. Cook, stirring frequently, until slightly thickened. Stir in tomatoes, steak sauce and pepper sauce, breaking up tomatoes. Heat to boiling; reduce heat. Simmer uncovered 10 to 15 minutes. Stir in rice; heat through.

1 Serving		% Daily Value:	
Calories	330	Vitamin A	10%
Calories from fat	100	Vitamin C	30%
Fat, g	11	Calcium	6%
Saturated, g	4	Iron	16%
Cholesterol, mg	80		
Sodium, mg	1000		
Carbohydrate, g	34		
Dietary Fiber, g	4		
Protein, g	28		

Turkey and Brown Rice Chili

6 SERVINGS

⏳ ⬇

Top this hearty chili with low-fat cheese, chopped green onions, cilantro or low-fat yogurt.

1 large onion, chopped (about 1 cup)

3/4 pound ground turkey breast

1 can (28 ounces) no-salt-added whole tomatoes, undrained

1 can (15 ounces) chili beans in sauce, undrained

1 can (4 ounces) chopped green chilies, drained

1 tablespoon sugar

1 tablespoon chili powder

1 teaspoon ground cumin

2 1/2 cups water

1 cup uncooked brown or regular long-grain white rice

Spray nonstick Dutch oven with nonstick cooking spray; heat over medium heat. Cook onion and ground turkey in Dutch oven, stirring frequently, until turkey is no longer pink; drain. Stir in remaining ingredients except water and rice, breaking up tomatoes. Cook uncovered 10 minutes. Stir water and rice into turkey mixture. Cover and cook 40 minutes. Uncover and cook 5 to 10 minutes longer or until rice is tender.

1 Serving		% Daily Value:	
Calories	275	Vitamin A	16%
Calories from fat	35	Vitamin C	34%
Fat, g	4	Calcium	8%
Saturated, g	1	Iron	20%
Cholesterol, mg	35		
Sodium, mg	500		
Carbohydrate, g	47		
Dietary Fiber, g	8		
Protein, g	21		

COOKING LIQUID OPTIONS

Using water to cook grains is only one of many possibilities! Other liquids can be very flavorful, especially for recipes in which the grain absorbs the liquid. Try any of the following liquids as a substitute for water:

- beef, chicken, turkey or vegetable broth
- apple, orange or fruit juice blends
- clam, tomato or vegetable juices
- wine or half wine and half water

Chicken with Gingered Brown Rice Stuffing

4 SERVINGS

[X] [I]

Crystallized ginger adds a spicy flavor to this easy chicken and rice dish.

1 tablespoon orange juice

1 small onion, finely chopped (about 1/4 cup)

2 cups cooked brown or white rice

3 tablespoons finely chopped crystallized ginger

2 tablespoons chopped fresh parsley or 2 teaspoons dried parsley flakes

1 tablespoon orange juice

3/4 teaspoon chopped fresh or 1/4 teaspoon dried thyme leaves

4 skinless, boneless chicken breast halves (1 pound)

1 tablespoon orange juice

1/4 teaspoon cinnamon

Heat oven to 350°. Heat 1 tablespoon orange juice to boiling in 2-quart saucepan over medium heat. Cook onion in orange juice, stirring frequently, until crisp-tender. Stir in rice, ginger, parsley, 1 tablespoon orange juice and the thyme. Spoon rice mixture into greased square baking dish, 8 × 8 × 2 inches.

Place chicken breasts over rice mixture; brush with 1 tablespoon orange juice; sprinkle with cinnamon. Cover and bake 30 minutes. Remove cover; bake 15 to 20 minutes longer or until juice of chicken is no longer pink when centers of thickest pieces are cut.

1 Serving		% Daily Value:	
Calories	240	Vitamin A	0%
Calories from fat	35	Vitamin C	6%
Fat, g	4	Calcium	2%
Saturated, g	1	Iron	8%
Cholesterol, mg	60		
Sodium, mg	70		
Carbohydrate, g	26		
Dietary Fiber, g	2		
Protein, g	27		

Chicken with Gingered Brown Rice Stuffing

Curried Chicken and Rice

4 SERVINGS

Everything is cooked in one skillet in this mildly flavored curry dish, making it easy for any night of the week.

2 teaspoons vegetable oil

2 teaspoons curry powder

1 pound skinless, boneless chicken breasts, cut into 1-inch cubes

1 medium onion, chopped (about 1/2 cup)

1 clove garlic, finely chopped

1 can (14 1/2 ounces) 1/3-less-salt clear chicken broth

3/4 cup uncooked jasmine or regular long-grain white rice

1/3 cup raisins

1/2 teaspoon paprika

Heat oil in 10-inch nonstick skillet over medium heat. Stir in curry powder. Stir in chicken, onion and garlic. Cook, stirring frequently, until chicken is light brown. Stir in broth, rice and raisins. Heat to boiling; reduce heat. Cover and simmer 15 to 20 minutes or until chicken is no longer pink in center and rice is tender. Sprinkle with paprika.

1 Serving		% Daily Value:	
Calories	320	Vitamin A	2%
Calories from fat	55	Vitamin C	2%
Fat, g	6	Calcium	4%
Saturated, g	2	Iron	16%
Cholesterol, mg	60		
Sodium, mg	240		
Carbohydrate, g	41		
Dietary Fiber, g	2		
Protein, g	28		

Creamy Chicken and Wild Rice Casserole

4 SERVINGS

2 tablespoons water

1 medium stalk celery, chopped (about 1/2 cup)

1 medium onion, chopped (about 1/2 cup)

1 small red or green bell pepper, chopped (about 1/2 cup)

1 cup sliced mushrooms (about 3 ounces)

1 can (10 3/4 ounces) condensed cream of chicken soup with reduced fat and salt

3/4 cup skim milk

2 cups cooked wild rice

1 cup cut-up cooked chicken (about 6 ounces)

3/4 teaspoon chopped fresh or 1/4 teaspoon dried thyme leaves

1/8 teaspoon pepper

1 can (8 ounces) sliced water chestnuts, drained

Heat oven to 350°. Heat water to boiling in 2-quart saucepan. Cook celery, onion, bell pepper and mushrooms in water, stirring frequently, until crisp-tender; remove from heat. Stir in soup and milk. Stir in remaining ingredients. Spoon into ungreased 2-quart casserole. Cover and bake 30 to 40 minutes or until hot and bubbly.

1 Serving		% Daily Value:	
Calories	240	Vitamin A	14%
Calories from fat	35	Vitamin C	24%
Fat, g	4	Calcium	10%
Saturated, g	1	Iron	12%
Cholesterol, mg	30		
Sodium, mg	670		
Carbohydrate, g	360		
Dietary Fiber, g	3		
Protein, g	18		

Ham and Swiss Casserole

4 SERVINGS

When it's a chilly night and time for comfort food, this flavorful, creamy casserole really fills the bill. If no-salt-added mushrooms are available in your area, use them to reduce sodium even further.

1 tablespoon margarine

2 tablespoons all-purpose flour

1 1/4 cups skim milk

2 cups cooked brown or white rice

1 1/4 cups cut-up fully cooked smoked reduced-fat ham (about 10 ounces)

1 cup shredded reduced-fat Swiss cheese (4 ounces)

1/4 cup chopped fresh parsley

1/2 teaspoon dried marjoram leaves

1 can (4 ounces) mushroom stems and pieces, drained

Heat oven to 350°. Spray 2-quart casserole with nonstick cooking spray. Melt margarine in 3-quart saucepan over low heat. Cook flour in margarine, stirring constantly, until thickened; remove from heat.

Stir milk into flour mixture. Heat to boiling, stirring constantly with wire whisk. Boil and stir 1 minute. Stir in remaining ingredients. Spoon into casserole. Bake uncovered 30 to 35 minutes or until hot and bubbly.

1 Serving		% Daily Value:	
Calories	350	Vitamin A	10%
Calories from fat	110	Vitamin C	16%
Fat, g	12	Calcium	46%
Saturated, g	5	Iron	12%
Cholesterol, mg	50		
Sodium, mg	1360		
Carbohydrate, g	33		
Dietary Fiber, g	3		
Protein, g	30		

Apple-Rosemary Pork and Barley

4 SERVINGS

Pork tenderloin, barley, fresh rosemary and apple juice combine in this sweet and savory skillet meal that tastes as if it took a long time to prepare!

1 1/2 cups apple juice

3/4 cup uncooked quick-cooking barley

1 tablespoon chopped fresh or 1 teaspoon crushed dried rosemary leaves

3/4 pound pork tenderloin

2 teaspoons vegetable oil

1 medium onion, chopped (about 1/2 cup)

1 clove garlic, finely chopped

1 tablespoon chopped fresh or 1 teaspoon crushed dried rosemary leaves

1/4 cup apple jelly

1 large unpeeled red cooking apple, sliced (about 1 1/2 cups)

Rosemary sprigs, if desired

Heat apple juice to boiling in 2-quart saucepan. Stir in barley and 1 tablespoon rosemary; reduce heat. Cover and simmer 20 to 25 minutes or until liquid is absorbed and barley is tender.

Meanwhile, trim fat from pork tenderloin. Cut pork into 1/4-inch slices. Heat oil in 10-inch nonstick skillet over medium-high heat. Cook pork, onion, garlic and 1 tablespoon rosemary in oil, stirring frequently, until pork is no longer pink. Stir in apple jelly and sliced apple; heat through. Serve over barley. Garnish with rosemary sprigs, if desired.

1 Serving		% Daily Value:	
Calories	370	Vitamin A	0%
Calories from fat	55	Vitamin C	6%
Fat, g	6	Calcium	4%
Saturated, g	2	Iron	14%
Cholesterol, mg	50		
Sodium, mg	50		
Carbohydrate, g	63		
Dietary Fiber, g	6		
Protein, g	22		

Ginger Pork and Kasha

4 SERVINGS

1/2 cup low-sodium teriyaki sauce

1 teaspoon grated gingerroot

1 clove garlic, finely chopped

3/4 pound lean pork boneless loin, cut into thin strips

1/2 cup uncooked roasted buckwheat kernels or groats (kasha)

1 egg white

1 cup boiling water

2 teaspoons vegetable oil

2 medium carrots, thinly sliced (about 1 cup)

1 medium green bell pepper, cut into 1-inch pieces

1/2 cup water

1 tablespoon cornstarch

Mix teriyaki sauce, gingerroot and garlic in large bowl. Stir in pork. Cover and refrigerate 20 to 30 minutes.

Meanwhile, mix buckwheat and egg white. Cook buckwheat mixture in 8-inch skillet over medium-high heat, stirring constantly, until kernels separate and dry. Transfer buckwheat to medium bowl. Pour 1 cup boiling water over buckwheat; let stand 10 to 15 minutes or until liquid is absorbed.

Remove pork from marinade; reserve marinade. Heat oil in 10-inch nonstick skillet over medium-high heat. Add pork; stir-fry about 5 minutes or until no longer pink. Add carrots; cover and cook 2 to 3 minutes or until crisp-tender. Add bell pepper; stir-fry about 2 to 3 minutes or until crisp-tender.

Mix reserved marinade, 1/2 cup water and the cornstarch; stir into pork mixture. Heat to boiling. Boil 1 minute, stirring frequently. Stir in buckwheat; heat through.

1 Serving		% Daily Value:	
Calories	220	Vitamin A	56%
Calories from fat	65	Vitamin C	16%
Fat, g	7	Calcium	2%
Saturated, g	2	Iron	8%
Cholesterol, mg	35		
Sodium, mg	575		
Carbohydrate, g	23		
Dietary Fiber, g	2		
Protein, g	18		

Quick and Easy Sweet-and-Sour Beef

4 SERVINGS

2 teaspoons vegetable oil

1/4 teaspoon ground ginger

3/4 pound beef sirloin steak, cut into thin strips

1 medium onion, chopped (about 1/2 cup)

1 clove garlic, finely chopped

1 medium green bell pepper, cut into 1-inch pieces

1 can (8 ounces) pineapple tidbits in juice, drained

1 jar (9 ounces) sweet-and-sour sauce (about 1 cup)

1 medium tomato, seeded and coarsely chopped (about 3/4 cup)

2 cups hot cooked brown or white rice

Heat oil and ginger in 10-inch nonstick skillet over medium-high heat. Add beef, onion and garlic; stir-fry about 5 minutes or until beef is no longer pink. Add bell pepper; stir-fry 2 minutes. Stir in pineapple and sweet-and-sour sauce; heat through. Gently stir in tomato. Serve over rice.

1 Serving		% Daily Value:	
Calories	310	Vitamin A	2%
Calories from fat	55	Vitamin C	24%
Fat, g	6	Calcium	4%
Saturated, g	1	Iron	14%
Cholesterol, mg	40		
Sodium, mg	470		
Carbohydrate, g	50		
Dietary Fiber, g	4		
Protein, g	18		

Baked Fish with Italian Rice

6 SERVINGS

Use your favorite fish for this easy baked dinner.

2 tablespoons water

1 medium onion, chopped (about 1/2 cup)

3 cups cooked brown or white rice

1 can (14 1/2 ounces) no-salt-added Italian-style stewed tomatoes, undrained

1 teaspoon Italian seasoning, crumbled

6 lean fish fillets, 1/4 inch thick (about 3/4 pound)

1 1/2 teaspoons olive or vegetable oil

1/2 teaspoon paprika

Heat oven to 400°. Heat water to boiling in 2 1/2-quart saucepan over medium-high heat. Cook onion in water, stirring occasionally, until crisp-tender. Stir in rice, tomatoes and Italian seasoning; heat through.

Spoon rice mixture into ungreased rectangular baking dish, 13×9×2 inches. Place fish fillets on rice mixture. Brush fish with oil. Sprinkle with paprika. Cover and bake 20 to 25 minutes or until fish flakes easily with fork.

1 Serving		% Daily Value:	
Calories	180	Vitamin A	6%
Calories from fat	25	Vitamin C	8%
Fat, g	3	Calcium	4%
Saturated, g	1	Iron	26%
Cholesterol, mg	30		
Sodium, mg	330		
Carbohydrate, g	27		
Dietary Fiber, g	3		
Protein, g	14		

Marinated-Pork Fried Rice

4 SERVINGS

1/2 pound pork tenderloin

1/4 cup unsweetened pineapple juice

**1/2 teaspoon grated gingerroot or
1/4 teaspoon ground ginger**

1/4 teaspoon red pepper sauce

1 clove garlic, crushed

1 medium onion, chopped (about 1/2 cup)

**1 small red bell pepper, chopped (about
1/2 cup)**

**2 tablespoons low-sodium soy sauce or fish
sauce**

3 cups cold cooked rice

chopped fresh chives, if desired

Trim fat from pork tenderloin. Cut pork into
1/2-inch cubes. Mix pork, pineapple juice, gingerroot, pepper sauce and garlic in glass or plastic
bowl. Cover and refrigerate at least 1 hour but no
longer than 12 hours.

Spray wok or 12-inch nonstick skillet with nonstick cooking spray. Heat wok until hot. Remove
pork from marinade; drain. Add pork to wok; stir-
fry 5 to 10 minutes or until no longer pink.
Remove pork from wok.

Add onion and bell pepper to wok; stir-fry about 8
minutes or until onion is tender. Stir in pork and
remaining ingredients. Cook about 10 minutes,
stirring constantly, until rice is hot and golden.
Sprinkle with chopped fresh chives and serve with
additional soy sauce if desired.

1 Serving		% Daily Value:	
Calories	265	Vitamin A	6%
Calories from fat	25	Vitamin C	20%
Fat, g	3	Calcium	2%
Saturated, g	1	Iron	14%
Cholesterol, mg	45		
Sodium, mg	790		
Carbohydrate, g	40		
Dietary Fiber, g	1		
Protein, g	20		

Lemony Seafood Risotto

4 TO **5** SERVINGS

Risotto is an Italian dish where rice is first browned in butter and then cooked in broth. Arborio rice is traditionally used because it cooks up to a wonderful creamy consistency.

2 teaspoons olive or vegetable oil

1/4 cup finely chopped shallots (about 2 large) or green onions

2 cloves garlic, finely chopped

1 cup uncooked arborio or regular medium-grain white rice

1/2 cup dry white wine or nonalcoholic white wine

2 cans (14 1/2 ounces each) 1/3-less-salt clear chicken broth

2 teaspoons olive or vegetable oil

1/2 pound bay scallops

1/2 pound raw medium shrimp, peeled and deveined

1 teaspoon grated lemon peel

2 tablespoons fresh chopped parsley

Heat 2 teaspoons oil in 12-inch nonstick skillet over medium-high heat. Cook shallots and garlic in oil, stirring frequently, until shallots are crisp-tender. Reduce heat to medium. Stir in rice. Cook, stirring frequently, until rice begins to brown. Stir in wine. Cook until liquid is absorbed.

Pour 1/2 cup of the broth over rice mixture. Cook uncovered, stirring occasionally, until liquid is absorbed. Continue cooking 15 to 20 minutes, adding broth 1/2 cup at a time and stirring occasionally, until rice is tender and creamy.

Meanwhile, heat 2 teaspoons oil in 10-inch skillet over medium heat. Cook scallops and shrimp in oil 4 to 5 minutes, stirring frequently, until shrimp are pink. Remove scallops and shrimp from skillet, using slotted spoon. Gently stir scallops, shrimp and lemon peel into cooked rice mixture. Sprinkle with parsley.

1 Serving		% Daily Value:	
Calories	305	Vitamin A	6%
Calories from fat	55	Vitamin C	4%
Fat, g	6	Calcium	10%
Saturated, g	1	Iron	26%
Cholesterol, mg	70		
Sodium, mg	580		
Carbohydrate, g	41		
Dietary Fiber, g	1		
Protein, g	23		

Lemony Seafood Risotto

Baked Spinach Polenta

6 SERVINGS

⧗ ⬦ ♥ 🔋 ⬇

6 cups water

2 teaspoons tomato paste

1 1/2 cups yellow cornmeal

2 cups chopped mushrooms (about 8 ounces)

1 medium onion, chopped (about 1/2 cup)

1/3 cup canned 1/3-less-salt clear chicken broth

1 teaspoon chopped fresh or 1/2 teaspoon dried dill weed

1/4 teaspoon pepper

1/8 teaspoon ground nutmeg

1 package (10 ounces) frozen chopped spinach, thawed and squeezed to drain

1/2 cup shredded part-skim mozzarella cheese (2 ounces)

Heat oven to 375°. Spray rectangular pan, 11 × 7 × 1 1/2 inches, with nonstick cooking spray. Heat water and tomato paste to boiling in 2-quart saucepan; reduce heat to medium-low. Stir in cornmeal. Simmer uncovered about 10 minutes, stirring frequently, until mixture thickens and pulls away from side of saucepan. Spread in pan.

Cook mushrooms, onion and broth in 10-inch skillet over medium heat about 10 minutes or until liquid has almost evaporated. Stir in remaining ingredients except cheese. Cook 2 to 3 minutes, stirring frequently, until spinach is hot. Spread spinach mixture over cornmeal mixture; sprinkle with cheese. Bake uncovered about 40 minutes or until hot and cheese is lightly browned.

1 Serving		% Daily Value:	
Calories	160	Vitamin A	28%
Calories from fat	20	Vitamin C	4%
Fat, g	2	Calcium	12%
Saturated, g	1	Iron	12%
Cholesterol, mg	5		
Sodium, mg	95		
Carbohydrate, g	32		
Dietary Fiber, g	3		
Protein, g	7		

Wild Rice Frittata

6 SERVINGS

1 tablespoon margarine

1 small green bell pepper, chopped (about 1/2 cup)

1 small red bell pepper, chopped (about 1/2 cup)

1 medium onion, chopped (about 1/2 cup)

1 1/2 cups cholesterol-free egg product

1/4 cup skimmed milk

1 cup cooked wild rice

1 cup shredded reduced-fat Swiss cheese (4 ounces)

Melt margarine in 10-inch nonstick skillet over medium heat. Cook bell peppers and onion in margarine, stirring frequently, until vegetables are crisp-tender.

Mix egg product, milk, wild rice and 1/2 cup of the cheese; pour over vegetables. Reduce heat to low. Cover and cook 15 to 20 minutes or until eggs are set; remove from heat. Sprinkle with remaining cheese. Cover and let stand about 5 minutes or until cheese is melted. Serve immediately.

1 Serving		% Daily Value:	
Calories	135	Vitamin A	12%
Calories from fat	45	Vitamin C	18%
Fat, g	5	Calcium	26%
Saturated, g	2	Iron	8%
Cholesterol, mg	5		
Sodium, mg	230		
Carbohydrate, g	11		
Dietary Fiber, g	1		
Protein, g	13		

Mexican Rice and Bean Bake

6 SERVINGS

Add a green salad to this simple meatless dish and dinner is ready.

2 cups cooked brown or white rice

1/4 cup cholesterol-free egg product

1 1/2 cups picante sauce

1 cup shredded reduced-fat Cheddar cheese (4 ounces)

1 can (15 to 16 ounces) pinto beans, drained

1/4 teaspoon chili powder

Heat oven to 350°. Spray square baking dish, 8 × 8 × 2 inches, with nonstick cooking spray. Mix rice, egg product, 1/2 cup of the picante sauce and 1/2 cup of the cheese; press in bottom of baking dish.

Mix beans and remaining 1 cup picante sauce; spoon over rice mixture. Sprinkle with remaining 1/2 cup cheese and the chili powder. Bake uncovered 30 to 35 minutes or until cheese is melted and bubbly. Let stand 5 minutes before serving.

1 Serving		% Daily Value:	
Calories	220	Vitamin A	38%
Calories from fat	45	Vitamin C	18%
Fat, g	5	Calcium	20%
Saturated, g	2	Iron	14%
Cholesterol, mg	10		
Sodium, mg	880		
Carbohydrate, g	38		
Dietary Fiber, g	8		
Protein, g	14		

Grains

What do wheat, rice, oats and corn have in common? All are classified as grains, but are known by their individual names. Flour, bread, pasta and rice are the most familiar grain products, but tremendous variety exists with varieties such as amaranth or quinoa that go beyond wheat and rice. Why not try new grains or consider new ideas with common grains? There are many good reasons to inspire you:

- Grains add terrific flavor, texture and variety to meals. Definitely not boring, grains bring exciting variety to both tried and true recipes as well as new ones.

- Grains are good for you! Grains offer the benefit of fiber, are low in fat, contain no cholesterol, and combined with low-fat dairy products or beans, peas or lentils, they provide high-quality protein. The new Food Pyramid Guidelines recommend 6 to 11 servings from the grains food group each day.

- Grains are inexpensive, easy to prepare and can be made ahead and stored.

Grains Glossary

Amaranth: A drought-resistant grain that once was one of the primary foods of the Aztecs of ancient Mexico. Amaranth seed is very tiny and can be milled into flour or puffed like rice or corn. The flavor of amaranth is sweet and nutlike. It has been called a "supergrain" because of its superior amino acid profile. Rich in lysine, one of the eight essential amino acids, its protein composition in more complete than other vegetable proteins. The seed also contains unusually high levels of calcium (six to seven times as much as wheat), iron, phosphorus, magnesium and potassium.

Arborio Rice (Italian Rice): Is from northern Italy's Piedmont region, and is the premium grade of Italian rice. It is a unique short, plump rice that absorbs a great deal of liquid without becoming soggy, making it ideal for dishes that need slow, gentle cooking such as risotto, paella and jambalaya. If unavailable in your area, regular medium-grain white rice can be substituted.

Basmati Rice: Is known for its delicious flavor, nutty aroma and firm consistency. Originally developed in the foothills of the Himalayas in northern India, it is grown in only a few parts of the world because of the special soil required for this unique rice.

Barley: Is one of the first grains ever cultivated. Pearl barley is the most commonly available and has the hull, most of the bran and some of the germ removed to shorten cooking time. It contains niacin, thiamin and potassium. One cup of cooked barley provides the same amount of protein as a glass of milk.

Brown Rice: Is unpolished, meaning the outer hull has been removed, but the germ and bran layers have not been "polished" off. This gives it a nutlike flavor and chewier texture than white rice. It is also a good source of fiber and thiamin.

Buckwheat Kernels: Are also called roasted buckwheat kernels or groats, they are hulled seeds of the buckwheat plant. Roasted groats are often called *kasha*. Although technically a fruit, buckwheat kernels are used as a grain. Buckwheat contains phosphorus, iron, potassium, vitamin E and B vitamins. It has a pungent flavor that can be overpowering. Buckwheat flour is usually mixed with all-purpose flour for pastas, pancakes, muffins and quick breads.

Converted (parboiled) Rice: Is a rice that has been steamed and pressure-cooked before milling, a process that forces residual nutrients into the kernel's heart, making it a bit higher in vitamin content than regular white rice.

Corn: Is sometimes forgotten as a grain because it is usually eaten as a vegetable. Whole kernel corn adds a naturally sweet flavor and a crunchy texture to breads, main dishes and side dishes. Paired with legumes or small amounts of animal protein from dairy products or eggs, corn provides a complete protein. **Cornmeal** is available either as yellow, white or blue depending on the type of corn used. Cornmeal is available in degerminated and whole-grain forms. As *degerminated* indicates, the germ and bran have been removed. This type is widely available at grocery stores. Stone-ground whole-grain cornmeal may be found in co-ops or health food stores. It contains the germ and the bran, which gives it more flavor, texture and fiber. **Grits** are coarsely ground from hulled kernels of corn by a dry milling process. **Hominy** is dried corn kernels from which the hull and germ have been removed. Hull removal is either done mechanically or by soaking kernels in slaked lime or lye. Hominy is sold both canned and softened like beans, or dried.

Couscous ("koos-koos"): The most tiny pasta, it is a staple of North African and some Middle Eastern cuisines. Couscous is a granular form of semolina, from which pasta is made, but is most often used in place of rice. Couscous is available in regular and precooked varieties. Precooked couscous is ready to eat in just five minutes. **See also Pasta Glossary p. 42.**

Continues

Instant (precooked) Rice: Is commercially cooked, rinsed and dehydrated before packaging, resulting in a very short cooking time. White, brown and wild rice are all available in this form.

Jasmine: Is an aromatic long-grain rice originally grown in Thailand. This rice is similar to regular long-grain white rice in appearance but is moister and more tender.

Millet: Is a small, round yellow seed that resembles whole mustard seed. When cooked, whole millet has a chewy texture and a mild flavor similar to brown rice. It is a very high-quality protein, is particularly high in minerals, and is thought to be the most digestible of all grains.

Oats: Oats eaten for breakfast as oatmeal are steamed and flattened groats (hulled oat kernels). They are available either as regular (old-fashioned), quick-cooking or instant. Regular and quick-cooking oats are often used interchangeably. If a recipe specifies just one type, do not substitute the other—they have different absorption properties. Oats contribute fiber, thiamin, phosphorus and magnesium to the diet.

Quinoa ("keen-wa"): Was once the staple food of the Inca Indians in Peru. It is a small grain with a soft crunch and can be used in any recipe calling for rice. Be sure to rinse it well before using to remove the bitter-tasting, naturally occurring saponin (nature's insect repellent) that forms on the outside of the kernel. Quinoa provides B vitamins, calcium, iron, phosphorus and, unlike other grains, is a complete protein.

Texmati Rice: Is a cross between basmati and regular long-grain white rice that is grown in the United States. Like basmati, it has a nutty flavor and aroma and is available as both white and brown.

White Rice (regular): Has been milled to remove the hull, germ and most of the bran. It is available in long, medium and short grains. The shorter the grain, the stickier the cooked rice will be. Long-grain is the most common all-purpose rice. Medium-grain works well in puddings because of its creamier characteristics. Short-grain white rice is not widely available.

Wild Rice: Is actually an aquatic grass native to North America. It is more expensive than other rices because of its limited supply. Stretch it by mixing with other rices or grains. Wild rice contains fiber, B vitamins, iron, phosphorus, magnesium, calcium and zinc.

Wheat Berries: Are hulled whole-grain wheat kernels that still have the bran and germ. Cooked wheat berries can be used like rice in salads and side dishes. Wheat provides B vitamins, vitamin E and complex carbohydrates.

Wheat Bulgur: Is whole wheat that has been cooked, dried and then broken into coarse fragments. It's different from cracked wheat because it is precooked. Bulgur supplies phosphorus and potassium and also contains some iron, thiamin and riboflavin.

Wheat Flour: Is available in several different forms. **Quick-mixing flour** is instant all-purpose flour, which means it disperses instantly in cold liquids, resulting in smooth gravies, sauces and batters. **Cake flour** is milled from soft wheat, which has a weaker gluten structure, creating tender cakes with greater volume. **All-purpose flour** is either milled from hard winter wheat or a blend of hard and soft winter wheats to provide a flour that produces acceptable results over a wide range of baked products. **Bread flour** is milled from hard winter wheat, hard spring wheat or a combination of the two and provides the gluten structure needed in yeast breads. Quick-mixing, cake, all-purpose and bread flours don't contain the bran or the germ of wheat. **Whole wheat flour** is ground from the whole wheat kernel, usually from hard spring wheat, and contains the nutrients of whole wheat berries.

Wheat Germ: Is the flaked embryo of the berry. Because it's high in oil, it is usually toasted, to extend its shelf life. It has a nutty flavor and can be sprinkled over cereal or used in baked goods. It is a good source of thiamin, niacin, riboflavin, potassium and zinc.

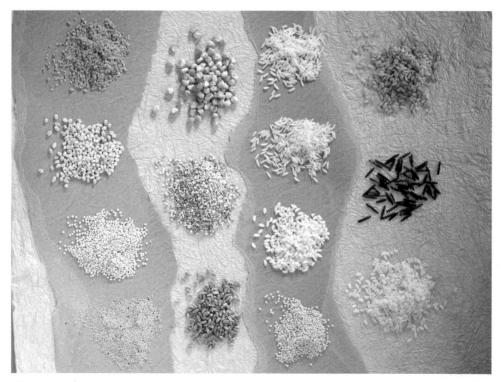

(From top to bottom)

Row 1: Bulgar, Barley, Quinoa, Amaranth
Row 2: Corn Kernel, Kasha, Wheat Berries
Row 3: Basmati Rice, Jasmine Rice, Arborio Rice, Millet
Row 4: Brown Rice, Wild Rice, White Rice

Tomato-Corn Quiche

6 SERVINGS

1 cup evaporated skimmed milk

1/2 cup cholesterol-free egg product

2 tablespoons all-purpose flour

1 tablespoon chopped fresh cilantro

1/2 teaspoon chili powder

1/4 teaspoon onion powder

1/4 teaspoon pepper

1/4 teaspoon salt

1 cup frozen whole kernel corn, thawed

3/4 cup shredded reduced-fat Cheddar cheese (3 ounces)

1 medium tomato, seeded and chopped (about 3/4 cup)

Heat oven to 350°. Spray pie plate, 9 × 1 1/4 inches, with nonstick cooking spray. Mix milk, egg product, flour, cilantro, chili and onion powder, salt and pepper in large bowl. Stir in remaining ingredients. Pour into pie plate.

Bake 35 to 45 minutes or until knife inserted in center comes out clean. Let stand 10 minutes before cutting.

1 Serving		% Daily Value:	
Calories	120	Vitamin A	10%
Calories from fat	25	Vitamin C	4%
Fat, g	3	Calcium	24%
Saturated, g	2	Iron	4%
Cholesterol, mg	10		
Sodium, mg	160		
Carbohydrate, g	14		
Dietary Fiber, g	1		
Protein, g	10		

REHEATING PASTA AND GRAINS

Leftover pasta or rice can be a real time-saver during the middle of the week when every minute counts to get an evening meal on the table.*

There are 3 ways to reheat leftover plain pasta and grains:

1. Place pasta or grain in rapidly boiling water for up to 2 minutes. Drain and serve immediately.

2. Place pasta or grain in colander and pour boiling water over it until heated through. Drain and serve immediately.

3. Place pasta or grain in microwave-safe dish or container. Microwave tightly covered on high for 1 to 3 minutes or until heated through. Serve immediately.

*See **Storage** sections of Grain and Pasta*

Lemon-Parsley Millet Pilaf

6 SERVINGS

1 can (14 1/2 ounces) 1/3-less-salt clear chicken broth

1/3 cup water

1/4 teaspoon onion powder

1/2 cup uncooked millet

1/2 cup uncooked regular long-grain white rice

1/2 cup frozen whole kernel corn

1/2 cup coarsely chopped fresh parsley

1 teaspoon grated lemon peel

Heat broth, water and onion powder to boiling in 2-quart saucepan. Stir in millet, rice and corn; reduce heat. Cover and simmer 16 to 18 minutes or until millet and rice are tender. Stir in parsley and lemon peel. Serve immediately.

1 Serving		% Daily Value:	
Calories	130	Vitamin A	2%
Calories from fat	10	Vitamin C	6%
Fat, g	1	Calcium	2%
Saturated, g	0	Iron	8%
Cholesterol, mg	0		
Sodium, mg	130		
Carbohydrate, g	28		
Dietary Fiber, g	2		
Protein, g	4		

Millet Pilaf

6 SERVINGS

1 medium onion, thinly sliced

1 medium green bell pepper, chopped (about 1 cup)

1 cup uncooked millet

3 cups water

1 tablespoon low-sodium chicken bouillon granules

1/8 teaspoon ground ginger

1 medium unpeeled apple, coarsely chopped (about 1 cup)

Spray 10-inch nonstick skillet with nonstick cooking spray. Cook onion, bell pepper and millet in skillet about 5 minutes over medium heat, stirring occasionally, until onion is crisp-tender.

Stir in water, bouillon granules and ginger. Heat to boiling; reduce heat. Cover and simmer about 15 to 20 minutes or until millet is tender. Stir in apple; heat through.

1 Serving		% Daily Value:	
Calories	155	Vitamin A	0%
Calories from fat	20	Vitamin C	10%
Fat, g	2	Calcium	2%
Saturated, g	1	Iron	6%
Cholesterol, mg	0		
Sodium, mg	5		
Carbohydrate, g	32		
Dietary Fiber, g	2		
Protein, g	4		

Indian Rice

6 SERVINGS

2 tablespoons water

1 small onion, chopped (about 1/4 cup)

1 cup uncooked basmati or regular long-grain white rice

2/3 cup raisins

2 cups water

2 tablespoons slivered almonds

1/2 teaspoon ground cinnamon

1/2 teaspoon salt

1/4 teaspoon ground turmeric

1/4 teaspoon pepper

Heat 2 tablespoons water to boiling in 2-quart saucepan over medium-high heat. Cook onion in water, stirring frequently until crisp-tender. Stir in remaining ingredients. Heat to boiling; reduce heat. Cover and simmer 15 to 20 minutes or until liquid is absorbed and rice is tender.

1 Serving		% Daily Value:	
Calories	185	Vitamin A	0%
Calories from fat	20	Vitamin C	0%
Fat, g	2	Calcium	2%
Saturated, g	0	Iron	8%
Cholesterol, mg	0		
Sodium, mg	180		
Carbohydrate, g	40		
Dietary Fiber, g	1		
Protein, g	3		

Seasoned Brown Rice

6 SERVINGS

This herb-flavored rice goes well with any type of meat, poultry or fish.

1 tablespoon margarine

1/3 cup chopped green onions (about 3 medium)

1 1/2 teaspoons chopped fresh or 1/2 teaspoon ground sage

3/4 teaspoon chopped fresh or 1/4 teaspoon dried oregano leaves

3/4 teaspoon chopped fresh or 1/4 teaspoon dried thyme leaves

1 cup uncooked brown or regular long-grain white rice

2 3/4 cups apple juice or water

1/4 teaspoon salt

Melt margarine in 2 1/2-quart nonstick saucepan over medium heat. Cook onions, sage, oregano and thyme in margarine, stirring frequently, until onions are crisp-tender. Stir in remaining ingredients. Heat to boiling; reduce heat. Cover and simmer 45 to 50 minutes or until liquid is absorbed and rice is tender.

1 Serving		% Daily Value:	
Calories	185	Vitamin A	2%
Calories from fat	25	Vitamin C	0%
Fat, g	3	Calcium	2%
Saturated, g	1	Iron	6%
Cholesterol, mg	0		
Sodium, mg	120		
Carbohydrate, g	38		
Dietary Fiber, g	2		
Protein, g	3		

Dilled Corn with Popped Amaranth

5 SERVINGS

⚊ ⚫ ♥ ⚊ ⚊

Popped amaranth adds a pleasant crunch to vegetables, salads and casseroles.

2 tablespoons uncooked amaranth

1 package (16 ounces) frozen whole kernel corn

1 tablespoon margarine

1 tablespoon chopped fresh or 1 teaspoon dried dill weed

Heat heavy skillet over medium-high heat until very hot. Heat 1 tablespoon of the amaranth in skillet 30 to 45 seconds, stirring constantly with wooden spoon, until most of the seeds pop. Remove from skillet. Repeat with remaining 1 tablespoon amaranth.

Cook and drain corn as directed on package. Stir in margarine and dill weed. Sprinkle with amaranth. Serve immediately.

1 Serving		% Daily Value:	
Calories	105	Vitamin A	4%
Calories from fat	25	Vitamin C	2%
Fat, g	3	Calcium	0%
Saturated, g	1	Iron	4%
Cholesterol, mg	0		
Sodium, mg	30		
Carbohydrate, g	21		
Dietary Fiber, g	4		
Protein, g	3		

TOASTING GRAINS

Toasting adds a special touch of flavor to foods. You are probably familiar with the heightened flavor and added texture of toasted nuts. This same delightful flavor can be achieved by toasting grains *before cooking.*

Amaranth, millet, oats, quinoa, unprocessed bran and wheat berries can be toasted by one of the following methods*:

Skillet Method: Sprinkle up to 1/2 cup grain in ungreased heavy skillet. Cook over medium heat 3 to 7 minutes, stirring frequently until grain begins to brown, then stirring constantly until golden brown.

Oven Method: Heat oven to 350°. Place up to 1/2 cup grain in shallow ungreased pan, stirring occasionally, until golden brown, 5 to 10 minutes.

Microwave Oven: Place up to 1/2 cup grain in microwave-safe pie plate and microwave on high 2 minutes 30 seconds to 3 minutes, stirring every 30 seconds until light brown. (Note: If using less than 1/2 cup grain, cooking times will be reduced. Microwave in 30-second intervals until light brown.)

Note that the toasting time for each grain will vary; watch closely so it doesn't get too dark or burn.

Risotto Primavera

8 SERVINGS

Primavera is an Italian term meaning "spring." Here, as with pasta, it refers to the fresh vegetables used in the dish.

2 teaspoons olive or vegetable oil

1 medium onion, chopped (about 1/2 cup)

1 small carrot, cut into julienne strips (about 1/2 cup)

1 cup uncooked arborio or regular medium-grain white rice

2 cans (14 1/2 ounces each) 1/3-less-salt clear chicken broth

1 cup broccoli flowerets

1 cup frozen green peas

1 small zucchini, cut into julienne strips (about 1/2 cup)

8 teaspoons grated Parmesan cheese

Heat oil in 3-quart nonstick saucepan over medium-high heat. Cook onion and carrot in oil, stirring frequently, until crisp-tender. Stir in rice. Cook, stirring frequently, until rice begins to brown.

Pour 1/2 cup of the broth over rice mixture. Cook uncovered, stirring occasionally, until liquid is absorbed. Continue cooking 15 to 20 minutes, adding broth 1/2 cup at a time and stirring occasionally, until rice is tender and creamy; add broccoli, peas and zucchini with the last addition of broth. Sprinkle with cheese.

1 Serving		% Daily Value:	
Calories	120	Vitamin A	14%
Calories from fat	20	Vitamin C	12%
Fat, g	2	Calcium	4%
Saturated, g	1	Iron	6%
Cholesterol, mg	0		
Sodium, mg	230		
Carbohydrate, g	24		
Dietary Fiber, g	2		
Protein, g	4		

Risotto Primavera

Cranberry–Wild Rice Bake

8 SERVINGS

1 cup uncooked wild rice

2 1/2 cups water

2 teaspoons margarine

1 medium onion, chopped (about 1/2 cup)

1 cup sliced mushrooms (about 3 ounces)

2 1/2 cups hot water

1 tablespoon low-sodium chicken bouillon granules

1/2 teaspoon garlic powder

1/4 teaspoon salt

1 cup dried cranberries

Heat oven to 350°. Place wild rice in wire strainer. Run cold water through rice, lifting rice with fingers to clean thoroughly. Heat rice and 2 1/2 cups water to boiling, stirring occasionally; reduce heat. Cover and simmer 30 minutes; drain. Melt margarine in 10-inch skillet over medium heat. Cook onion and mushrooms in margarine, stirring frequently until onion is tender.

Mix wild rice and onion mixture in greased square baking dish, 8 × 8 × 2 inches. Mix hot water, bouillon granules, garlic powder and salt; pour over rice mixture. Cover and bake 1 1/4 hours. Stir in cranberries. Cover and bake 15 to 20 minutes or until liquid is absorbed.

1 Serving		% Daily Value:	
Calories	120	Vitamin A	2%
Calories from fat	20	Vitamin C	2%
Fat, g	2	Calcium	0%
Saturated, g	0	Iron	4%
Cholesterol, mg	0		
Sodium, mg	80		
Carbohydrate, g	23		
Dietary Fiber, g	2		
Protein, g	4		

Fruit and Nut Quinoa

5 SERVINGS

3/4 cup uncooked quinoa

2 teaspoons margarine

1/4 cup finely chopped shallots (about 2 large) or green onions

1/4 cup finely chopped green bell pepper

1/2 cup chopped dried apricots

1/4 cup golden raisins

2 tablespoons chopped walnuts

1/4 teaspoon ground allspice

Dash of salt

Cook quinoa as directed on page 110. Meanwhile, melt margarine in 2 1/2-quart saucepan over medium-high heat. Cook shallots and bell pepper in margarine, stirring frequently, until tender. Stir in quinoa and remaining ingredients; heat through.

1 Serving		% Daily Value:	
Calories	195	Vitamin A	20%
Calories from fat	45	Vitamin C	12%
Fat, g	5	Calcium	2%
Saturated, g	1	Iron	18%
Cholesterol, mg	0		
Sodium, mg	80		
Carbohydrate, g	35		
Dietary Fiber, g	2		
Protein, g	5		

Fruit and Nut Quinoa

Selection, Storage and Preparation
Grains Primer

Selection

Corn, oats, rice and wheat are widely available in supermarkets, while others are also found in the health food section of large supermarkets, co-ops, health food stores and specialty food mail-order catalogs. Grains are often sold in bulk form or are packaged and sold in a refrigerator case. When selecting grains for occasional use, purchase in small quantities, if possible.

Storage

Uncooked Grains: Most grains can be stored indefinitely, but for optimum quality and flavor, a 1- to 2-year storage time is recommended.

- Store in original packaging or transfer to airtight glass or plastic containers and label contents with starting storage date.

- Store in a cool (60° or less), dry location. All grains can be refrigerated or frozen, which is a good idea if you live in a hot, humid climate. Whole grains that contain oil (brown rice, stone-ground or whole-grain cornmeal, wheat berries, wheat germ and whole wheat flour) can become rancid and *must be stored in the refrigerator or freezer*; store up to 6 months.

Cooked Grains:

Refrigerator: Cooked grains can be covered and stored in the refrigerator for up to 5 days.

Freezer: Cooked grains can be frozen in airtight containers for up to 6 months.

Preparation

Rinsing grains before cooking is not necessary with the exception of quinoa. Grains lose moisture with age, so more liquid may be needed than the recipe calls for. If all the liquid is absorbed but the grain isn't quite tender, add a little more liquid and cook longer. If tender but all liquid hasn't absorbed, just drain. Grains soaked in boiling water may need a longer soaking time or additional boiling water to soften completely.

See Grains Cooking Chart, page 108.

Turkey-Vegetable–Wild Rice Soup

6 SERVINGS

✶ ✶

Homemade broth is easy! Store your turkey carcass and bones in the freezer until you're ready to make the soup.

Broth (right) or 6 cups chicken broth

2 tablespoons water

2 cups sliced mushrooms (about 6 ounces)

2 medium stalks celery, sliced (about 1 cup)

1 medium onion, chopped (about 1/2 cup)

1/4 cup all-purpose flour

1 tablespoon chopped fresh or 1 teaspoon dried thyme leaves

3/4 teaspoon salt

1/4 teaspoon freshly ground pepper

3 cups cooked wild rice

2 cups cut-up cooked turkey (about 12 ounces)

1 1/2 cups frozen whole kernel corn

2 medium carrots, coarsely chopped (about 1 cup)

Prepare Broth. Heat water to boiling in 5-quart nonstick Dutch oven over medium-high heat. Cook mushrooms, celery and onion in water, stirring frequently, until onion is tender. Stir in flour, thyme, salt and pepper. Stir in broth and remaining ingredients. Heat to boiling; reduce heat. Cover and simmer 10 to 15 minutes, or until vegetables are tender.

Broth

ABOUT 6 CUPS BROTH

Carcass and bones from 12-pound turkey

2 medium stalks celery, sliced (about 1 cup)

1 medium onion, coarsely chopped (about 1/2 cup)

Place turkey carcass and bones, celery and onion in 5-quart Dutch oven. Add enough water to cover. Heat to boiling; reduce heat. Cover and simmer 2 to 3 hours. Drain, reserving broth. Remove any meat from bones and cut into small pieces; reserve for soup. Discard bones, celery and onion. Skim fat from broth.

1 Serving		% Daily Value:	
Calories	285	Vitamin A	38%
Calories from fat	45	Vitamin C	4%
Fat, g	5	Calcium	14%
Saturated, g	0	Iron	18%
Cholesterol, mg	40		
Sodium, mg	630		
Carbohydrate, g	41		
Dietary Fiber, g	4		
Protein, g	23		

Creamy Broccoli-Rice Soup

4 SERVINGS

This soup uses a calorie- and fat-saving technique to achieve its creaminess, without using cream. Our secret? Pureeing the vegetable mixture in a blender or food processor.

1/3 cup water

3 cups broccoli flowerets

1 medium onion, chopped (about 1/2 cup)

2 cans (14 1/2 ounces each) ready-to-serve vegetable broth or 1/3-less-salt clear chicken broth

1/2 cup uncooked brown or regular long-grain white rice

1 cup skimmed milk

1 teaspoon chopped fresh or 1/4 teaspoon dried oregano leaves

1/2 teaspoon salt

1/4 teaspoon pepper

Heat water to boiling in 3-quart saucepan over medium heat. Add broccoli and onion. Boil uncovered about 6 to 8 minutes or until almost tender. Drain and set aside. Heat broth and rice to boiling; reduce heat. Cover and simmer 18 to 20 minutes or until rice is tender.

Place half the broccoli mixture and half the broth mixture in food processor or blender. Cover and process until smooth; return Creamy Broccoli-Rice Soup to saucepan. Repeat with other half. Return broccoli mixture to saucepan. Stir in remaining ingredients; heat through.

1 Serving		% Daily Value:	
Calories	255	Vitamin A	58%
Calories from fat	45	Vitamin C	56%
Fat, g	5	Calcium	14%
Saturated, g	2	Iron	12%
Cholesterol, mg	40		
Sodium, mg	780		
Carbohydrate, g	39		
Dietary Fiber, g	6		
Protein, g	20		

Creamy Vegetable-Cheese Soup

8 SERVINGS

4 ounces light process cheese spread loaf, cubed

3 1/2 cups skimmed milk

1/2 teaspoon chili powder

2 cups cooked brown or white rice

1 package (16 ounces) frozen cauliflower, carrots and asparagus, thawed and drained

Heat cheese and milk in 3-quart saucepan or Dutch oven over low heat until cheese is melted. Stir in chili powder. Stir in rice and vegetables; heat through.

1 Serving		% Daily Value:	
Calories	140	Vitamin A	50%
Calories from fat	25	Vitamin C	14%
Fat, g	3	Calcium	26%
Saturated, g	2	Iron	2%
Cholesterol, mg	10		
Sodium, mg	420		
Carbohydrate, g	21		
Dietary Fiber, g	2		
Protein, g	9		

Creamy Broccoli-Rice Soup

Quick Beef-Barley Soup

6 SERVINGS

5 cups water

5 teaspoons low-sodium beef bouillon
granules

1 package (16 ounces) frozen sweet peas,
potatoes and carrots

1/2 cup uncooked quick-cooking barley

1 tablespoon chopped fresh or 1 teaspoon
dried marjoram leaves

1/4 teaspoon salt

1/4 cup water

2 tablespoons all-purpose flour

1 cup cubed cooked beef (about 8 ounces)

Heat 5 cups water to boiling in 3-quart saucepan.
Stir in bouillon granules until dissolved. Stir in
frozen vegetables, barley, marjoram and salt;
reduce heat. Cover and simmer about 10 minutes
or until barley is tender.

Mix 1/4 cup water and the flour; stir into barley
mixture. Cook until slightly thickened. Stir in
beef; heat through.

1 Serving		% Daily Value:	
Calories	195	Vitamin A	2%
Calories from fat	55	Vitamin C	4%
Fat, g	6	Calcium	2%
Saturated, g	2	Iron	10%
Cholesterol, mg	15		
Sodium, mg	150		
Carbohydrate, g	30		
Dietary Fiber, g	5		
Protein, g	10		

Tropical Fruit, Rice and Tuna Salad

4 SERVINGS

1 1/2 cups cold cooked brown or white rice

1/2 cup vanilla low-fat yogurt

1 can (8 ounces) pineapple tidbits in juice,
drained and 1 teaspoon juice reserved

2 kiwifruit, peeled and cut up

1 medium mango, peeled and chopped
(about 1 cup)

1 can (6 1/8 ounces) white tuna in water,
drained and flaked

1 tablespoon coconut, toasted

Mix rice, yogurt and reserved pineapple juice in
medium bowl. Cover and refrigerate 1 to 2 hours
to blend flavors. Cut kiwifruit slices into fourths.
Gently stir kiwifruit, pineapple, mango and tuna
into rice mixture. Sprinkle with coconut.

1 Serving		% Daily Value:	
Calories	240	Vitamin A	18%
Calories from fat	20	Vitamin C	44%
Fat, g	2	Calcium	8%
Saturated, g	1	Iron	8%
Cholesterol, mg	15		
Sodium, mg	170		
Carbohydrate, g	45		
Dietary Fiber, g	4		
Protein, g	15		

Tropical Fruit, Rice and Tuna Salad

GRAINS COOKING CHART

Type of Grain (1 cup uncooked amount)	Amount of Cooking Liquid (in cups)	Method of Cooking/ Preparation (using 2-quart saucepan with lid)
Arborio is used as an ingredient rice and is not generally cooked as a plain rice side dish. For recipes using this rice see pages 84 and 98.	Does not apply	Does not apply
Barley (quick-cooking)	2	Heat liquid to a boil. Stir in barley. Reduce heat. Cover and simmer.
Barley (regular)	4	Heat liquid to a boil. Stir in barley. Reduce heat. Cover and simmer.
Basmati Rice	1 1/2	Rinse rice thoroughly with cold water. Heat liquid to a boil. Stir in rice. Reduce heat. Cover and simmer.
Brown Rice	2 3/4	Heat rice and liquid to a boil. Reduce heat. Cover and simmer.
Bulgur	3	Pour boiling liquid over bulgur. Cover and soak. Drain if needed. Do not cook.
Couscous	1 1/2	Heat liquid to a boil. Stir in couscous. Cover and remove from heat.
Jasmine and Texmati Rice	1 3/4	Heat rice and liquid to a boil. Reduce heat. Cover and simmer.

Approximate Cooking Time in Minutes	Approximate Yield (in cups)
Does not apply	Does not apply
10 to 12 minutes. Let stand covered 5 minutes.	3
45 to 50 minutes. Let stand covered 5 minutes.	4
15 to 20 minutes.	3
45 to 50	4
Soak 30 to 60 minutes.	3
Let stand covered 5 minutes.	3 to 3 1/2
15 to 20	3

GRAINS COOKING CHART *(Continued)*

Type of Grain (1 cup uncooked amount)	Amount of Cooking Liquid (in cups)	Method of Cooking/ Preparation (using 2-quart saucepan with lid)
Kasha (roasted buckwheat kernels)	2	Pour boiling liquid over kasha. Cover and soak. Drain if needed. Or, cook according to package directions.
Millet	2 1/2	Heat millet and liquid to a boil. Reduce heat. Cover and simmer.
Parboiled Rice (converted)	2 1/2	Heat liquid to a boil. Stir in rice. Reduce heat. Cover and simmer.
Pre-cooked Brown Rice (instant)	1 1/4	Heat liquid to a boil. Stir in rice. Reduce heat. Cover and simmer.
Pre-cooked White Rice (instant)	1	Heat liquid to a boil. Stir in rice. Cover and remove from heat.
Quinoa	2	Heat quinoa and liquid to a boil. Reduce heat. Cover and simmer.
Regular Rice	2	Heat rice and liquid to a boil. Reduce heat. Cover and simmer.
Wheat Berries	2 1/2	Heat wheat berries and liquid to a boil. Reduce heat. Cover and simmer.
Wild Rice	2 1/2	Heat rice and liquid to a boil. Reduce heat. Cover and simmer.

Approximate Cooking Time in Minutes	Approximate Yield (in cups)
Soak 10 to 15 minutes.	4
15 to 20	4
20 minutes. Remove from heat. Let stand covered 5 minutes.	3 to 4
10	2
Let stand covered 5 minutes.	2
15	3 to 4
15	3
50 to 60	2 3/4 to 3
40 to 50	3

Ham and Brown Rice Salad

4 SERVINGS

- 3/4 cup nonfat mayonnaise or salad dressing
- 1/4 cup orange juice
- 2 cups cold cooked brown or white rice
- 1 cup chopped fully cooked smoked reduced-sodium ham (about 1/2 pound)
- 1 medium stalk celery, cut into 1/4-inch diagonal slices (about 1/2 cup)
- 1 can (11 ounces) mandarin orange segments, drained
- 2 tablespoons slivered almonds, toasted

Mix mayonnaise and orange juice in medium bowl. Stir in rice, ham and celery. Gently stir in orange segments. Sprinkle with almonds.

1 Serving		% Daily Value:	
Calories	235	Vitamin A	0%
Calories from fat	35	Vitamin C	52%
Fat, g	4	Calcium	4%
Saturated, g	2	Iron	8%
Cholesterol, mg	10		
Sodium, mg	870		
Carbohydrate, g	43		
Dietary Fiber, g	3		
Protein, g	10		

Tabbouleh

6 SERVINGS

- 3/4 cup uncooked bulgur
- 3 medium tomatoes, chopped (about 2 1/4 cups)
- 1 1/2 cups chopped fresh parsley
- 1/3 cup chopped green onions (about 3 medium)
- 2 tablespoons chopped fresh or 2 teaspoons crushed dried mint leaves
- 1/4 cup lemon juice
- 2 tablespoons olive or vegetable oil
- 1/4 teaspoon salt
- 1/4 teaspoon pepper

Cover bulgur with cold water; let stand 30 minutes. Drain bulgur; press out as much water as possible. Place bulgur, tomatoes, parsley, onions and mint in glass or plastic bowl. Mix remaining ingredients. Pour over bulgur mixture; toss. Cover and refrigerate 1 to 2 hours to blend flavors. Garnish with ripe olives if desired.

1 Serving		% Daily Value:	
Calories	110	Vitamin A	12%
Calories from fat	45	Vitamin C	58%
Fat, g	5	Calcium	4%
Saturated, g	1	Iron	10%
Cholesterol, mg	0		
Sodium, mg	110		
Carbohydrate, g	18		
Dietary Fiber, g	5		
Protein, g	3		

Spanish Rice Salad

6 SERVINGS

1 tablespoon olive or vegetable oil

1/2 cup finely chopped red onion (about
    1/2 medium)

1 clove garlic, crushed

1 1/2 cups uncooked brown rice

1/4 teaspoon ground turmeric

1/4 teaspoon crushed red pepper

2 cans (14 1/2 ounces each) 1/3-less-salt
    clear chicken broth

1 cup frozen green peas

1/2 cup sliced ripe olives

1 medium tomato, cut into wedges

1 small red bell pepper, chopped (about
    1/2 cup)

1 can (15 to 16 ounces) garbanzo beans,
    rinsed and drained

1 package (9 ounces) frozen artichoke
    hearts, thawed, drained and cut in half

1/2 cup spicy or regular tomato juice

2 tablespoons lemon juice

Lemon wedges, if desired

Heat oil in 2-quart saucepan over medium heat. Cook onion and garlic in oil 2 to 3 minutes, stirring frequently, until onion begins to soften. Stir in rice, turmeric and red pepper; stir to coat rice with oil. Stir in broth. Heat to boiling; reduce heat. Cover and simmer 45 to 50 minutes or until rice is tender.

Carefully mix rice mixture and remaining ingredients except tomato juice, lemon juice and lemon wedges in large bowl. Pour tomato and lemon juices over rice mixture; toss. Cover and refrigerate 2 to 3 hours to blend flavors. Serve with lemon wedges.

1 Serving		% Daily Value:	
Calories	350	Vitamin A	10%
Calories from fat	65	Vitamin C	50%
Fat, g	7	Calcium	8%
Saturated, g	1	Iron	24%
Cholesterol, mg	0		
Sodium, mg	660		
Carbohydrate, g	68		
Dietary Fiber, g	0		
Protein, g	14		

Wild Rice–Turkey Salad With Raspberry Vinaigrette

6 SERVINGS

3 cups cold cooked wild rice

1 1/2 cups cubed cooked turkey (about 9 ounces)

1/4 cup chopped green onions (2 to 3 medium)

1 medium green bell pepper, chopped (about 1 cup)

1 can (8 ounces) sliced water chestnuts, drained

1 package (6 ounces) diced dried fruits and raisins

1/3 cup raspberry vinegar

1/4 cup honey

2 tablespoons vegetable oil

Mix all ingredients except vinegar, honey and oil in large bowl. Shake vinegar, honey and oil in tightly covered container. Pour over wild rice mixture; toss. Cover and refrigerate 1 to 2 hours to blend flavors.

1 Serving		% Daily Value:	
Calories	325	Vitamin A	8%
Calories from fat	65	Vitamin C	24%
Fat, g	7	Calcium	2%
Saturated, g	1	Iron	12%
Cholesterol, mg	30		
Sodium, mg	40		
Carbohydrate, g	54		
Dietary Fiber, g	4		
Protein, g	15		

Wheat Berry Salad

4 SERVINGS

1 cup uncooked wheat berries

2 1/2 cups water

1 1/2 cups broccoli flowerets

1/2 cup chopped green onions (about 5 medium)

1 medium carrot, chopped (about 1/2 cup)

1 can (15 to 16 ounces) garbanzo beans, rinsed and drained

Vinaigrette Dressing (below)

Heat wheat berries and water to boiling in 2-quart saucepan, stirring occasionally; reduce heat. Cover and simmer 50 to 60 minutes or until wheat berries are tender but still chewy; drain. Toss wheat berries and remaining ingredients. Cover and refrigerate 1 to 2 hours to blend flavors.

Vinaigrette Dressing

1/4 cup balsamic or cider vinegar

1 tablespoon chopped fresh or 1 teaspoon dried basil leaves

2 tablespoons olive or vegetable oil

1/4 teaspoon paprika

1/8 teaspoon salt

1 clove garlic, crushed

Mix all ingredients.

1 Serving		% Daily Value:	
Calories	335	Vitamin A	34%
Calories from fat	90	Vitamin C	60%
Fat, g	10	Calcium	10%
Saturated, g	2	Iron	28%
Cholesterol, mg	0		
Sodium, mg	350		
Carbohydrate, g	57		
Dietary Fiber, g	11		
Protein, g	15		

Wild Rice–Corn Muffins

12 *MUFFINS*

Flecked with bits of wild rice and dried cranberries, these muffins are especially nice with roast turkey or chicken.

3/4 cup skim milk

1/4 cup vegetable oil

1/4 cup cholesterol-free egg product

1 cup all-purpose flour

1/2 cup sugar

1/2 cup yellow cornmeal

2 1/2 teaspoons baking powder

1/4 teaspoon salt

3/4 cup cooked wild rice

1/2 cup chopped fresh or frozen cranberries

Heat oven to 400°. Spray 12 medium muffin cups, 2 1/2 × 1 1/4 inches, with nonstick cooking spray, or line with paper baking cups. Mix milk, oil and egg product in large bowl. Stir in flour, sugar, cornmeal, baking powder and salt all at once just until flour is moistened. Fold in wild rice and cranberries.

Divide batter evenly among muffin cups. Bake 20 to 25 minutes or until golden brown. Immediately remove from pan. Serve warm.

1 Serving		% Daily Value:	
Calories	155	Vitamin A	0%
Calories from fat	45	Vitamin C	0%
Fat, g	5	Calcium	8%
Saturated, g	1	Iron	6%
Cholesterol, mg	0		
Sodium, mg	195		
Carbohydrate, g	25		
Dietary Fiber, g	1		
Protein, g	3		

Harvest Salad

8 SERVINGS

This tasty, colorful salad features fall's bounty, though it's delicious whenever you make it.

2 cups cooked barley

2 cups frozen whole kernel corn, thawed

1/2 cup dried cranberries

1/4 cup thinly sliced green onions (2 to 3 medium)

1 medium unpeeled apple, chopped (about 1 cup)

1 small carrot, coarsely shredded (about 1/3 cup)

2 tablespoons vegetable oil

2 tablespoons honey

1 tablespoon lemon juice

Mix all ingredients except oil, honey and lemon juice in large bowl. Shake oil, honey and lemon juice in tightly covered container. Pour over barley mixture; toss.

1 Serving		% Daily Value:	
Calories	150	Vitamin A	11%
Calories from fat	35	Vitamin C	10%
Fat, g	4	Calcium	0%
Saturated, g	1	Iron	2%
Cholesterol, mg	0		
Sodium, mg	25		
Carbohydrate, g	29		
Dietary Fiber, g	4		
Protein, g	3		

Spicy Pear and Bulgur Salad

8 SERVINGS

This salad is terrific served with pork for a main dish meal. And, for some delicious variety, try this bulgur and fruit combination for breakfast!

2 cups cooked bulgur

2 medium pears, peeled and coarsely chopped (about 2 cups)

1/2 cup raisins

1/4 cup orange juice

2 tablespoons packed brown sugar

1 teaspoon ground cinnamon

Mix bulgur, pears and raisins in large bowl. Shake orange juice, brown sugar and cinnamon in tightly covered container. Pour over bulgur mixture; toss. Cover and refrigerate 1 to 2 hours to blend flavors.

1 Serving		% Daily Value:	
Calories	100	Vitamin A	0%
Calories from fat	0	Vitamin C	8%
Fat, g	0	Calcium	2%
Saturated, g	0	Iron	4%
Cholesterol, mg	0		
Sodium, mg	280		
Carbohydrate, g	27		
Dietary Fiber, g	4		
Protein, g	2		

Harvest Salad, Wild Rice–Corn Muffins (page 115)

Vegetable-Kasha Salad with Balsamic Vinaigrette

4 SERVINGS

⧗ ♥

1/2 cup uncooked roasted buckwheat kernels or groats (kasha)

1 egg white

1 cup boiling water

1/4 cup thinly sliced green onions (2 to 3 medium)

2 medium tomatoes, seeded and coarsely chopped (about 1 1/2 cups)

1 medium unpeeled cucumber, seeded and chopped (about 1 1/4 cups)

Balsamic Vinaigrette (below)

Mix buckwheat and egg white. Cook buckwheat mixture in 8-inch skillet over medium-high heat, stirring constantly, until kernels separate and dry. Cook according to package directions; cool.

Mix buckwheat, onions, tomatoes and cucumber in large bowl. Pour Balsamic Vinaigrette over buckwheat mixture; toss. Cover and refrigerate 1 to 2 hours to blend flavors.

Balsamic Vinaigrette

1 tablespoon olive or vegetable oil

1 tablespoon balsamic or red wine vinegar

1 teaspoon sugar

1/4 teaspoon salt

1/8 teaspoon pepper

1 clove garlic, finely chopped

Shake all ingredients in tightly covered container.

1 Serving		% Daily Value:	
Calories	110	Vitamin A	4%
Calories from fat	35	Vitamin C	26%
Fat, g	4	Calcium	2%
Saturated, g	1	Iron	4%
Cholesterol, mg	0		
Sodium, mg	160		
Carbohydrate, g	17		
Dietary Fiber, g	2		
Protein, g	3		

Vegetable-Kasha Salad with Balsamic Vinaigrette

Creamy Rice-Fruit Salad

8 SERVINGS

Leftover cooked rice is just right for this easy salad.

1 kiwifruit, pared and cut into 1/4-inch slices

1 container (8 ounces) lemon or orange low-fat yogurt

1 tablespoon honey

2 cups cold cooked wild or brown rice

1 cup strawberries, cut in half

1/2 cup seedless green grapes, cut in half

1 teaspoon chopped fresh or 1/4 teaspoon dried mint leaves

1 medium seedless orange, cut into 1-inch pieces (about 1 cup)

Cut kiwifruit slices into fourths. Mix yogurt and honey in medium bowl. Add kiwifruit and remaining ingredients; toss. Refrigerate remaining salad.

1 Serving		% Daily Value:	
Calories	115	Vitamin A	0%
Calories from fat	10	Vitamin C	50%
Fat, g	1	Calcium	6%
Saturated, g	1	Iron	4%
Cholesterol, mg	0		
Sodium, mg	170		
Carbohydrate, g	25		
Dietary Fiber, g	1		
Protein, g	2		

Quinoa and Artichoke Salad

6 SERVINGS

2 cups cold cooked quinoa

1/4 cup thinly sliced green onions (2 to 3 medium)

1/4 cup nonfat Italian dressing

1/4 teaspoon garlic powder

1 small stalk celery, chopped (about 1/4 cup)

1 can (14 ounces) artichoke hearts, drained and coarsely chopped

2 medium tomatoes, seeded and chopped (about 1 1/2 cups)

2 tablespoons grated Parmesan cheese

Mix all ingredients except tomatoes and cheese. Cover and refrigerate 1 to 2 hours to blend flavors. Stir in tomatoes before serving. Sprinkle with cheese.

1 Serving		% Daily Value:	
Calories	145	Vitamin A	18%
Calories from fat	20	Vitamin C	22%
Fat, g	2	Calcium	4%
Saturated, g	0	Iron	18%
Cholesterol, mg	0		
Sodium, mg	60		
Carbohydrate, g	26		
Dietary Fiber, g	0		
Protein, g	6		

Creamy Rice-Fruit Salad

3

Bountiful Beans

∽

Vegetarian Chili (page 164)

Chicken in Peanut Sauce

4 SERVINGS

Inspired by an African stew, this recipe uses the common peanut, which is known as the groundnut in Africa.

3/4 pound skinless, boneless chicken breasts, cut into 1/2-inch pieces

1 medium onion, chopped (about 1/2 cup)

1 medium carrot, chopped (about 1/2 cup)

1 small green bell pepper, chopped (about 1/2 cup)

1/4 teaspoon garlic salt

1 can (14 1/2 ounces) no-salt-added whole tomatoes, undrained

1/2 cup water

2 tablespoons reduced-fat peanut butter

1/4 teaspoon chili powder

1 can (15 to 16 ounces) pinto beans, rinsed and drained

2 cups hot cooked rice

2 tablespoons chopped dry-roasted peanuts

Spray 12-inch nonstick skillet with nonstick cooking spray; heat over medium-high heat. Cook chicken, onion, carrot and bell pepper in skillet, stirring frequently, until chicken is no longer pink in center and vegetables are crisp-tender. Sprinkle with garlic salt.

Stir in tomatoes, water, peanut butter and chili powder, breaking up tomatoes. Stir in beans. Heat to boiling; reduce heat. Cover and simmer 10 minutes. Simmer uncovered 5 minutes longer. Serve over rice. Sprinkle with peanuts.

1 Serving		% Daily Value:	
Calories	430	Vitamin A	36%
Calories from fat	90	Vitamin C	26%
Fat, g	10	Calcium	12%
Saturated, g	2	Iron	30%
Cholesterol, mg	45		
Sodium, mg	740		
Carbohydrate, g	62		
Dietary Fiber, g	11		
Protein, g	34		

Southern Chicken Stir-fry

4 SERVINGS

Corn and black-eyed peas, seasoned with thyme and ground red pepper, make a southern-style stir-fry.

3/4 pound skinless, boneless chicken breast, cut into 1-inch pieces

1 cup cold cooked white rice

1 cup frozen whole kernel corn

1 1/2 teaspoons chopped fresh or 1/2 teaspoon dried thyme leaves

1/4 teaspoon salt

1/4 teaspoon garlic powder

1/8 teaspoon ground red pepper (cayenne)

1 can (15 to 16 ounces) black-eyed peas, rinsed and drained

2 cups packed fresh spinach leaves

Spray 12-inch nonstick skillet with nonstick cooking spray; heat over medium-high heat. Cook chicken in skillet, stirring occasionally, until no longer pink in center. Stir in remaining ingredients except spinach. Cook, stirring occasionally, until hot. Stir in spinach. Cook until spinach begins to wilt.

1 Serving		% Daily Value:	
Calories	265	Vitamin A	24%
Calories from fat	25	Vitamin C	8%
Fat, g	3	Calcium	6%
Saturated, g	1	Iron	28%
Cholesterol, mg	45		
Sodium, mg	610		
Carbohydrate, g	43		
Dietary Fiber, g	12		
Protein, g	29		

Easy Cassoulet

8 SERVINGS

1 pound fully cooked reduced-fat turkey kielbasa sausage, cut diagonally into 1-inch pieces

1 can (15 to 16 ounces) great northern beans, rinsed and drained

1 can (15 to 16 ounces) kidney beans, rinsed and drained

1 can (15 ounces) black beans, rinsed and drained

2 cans (8 ounces each) no-salt-added tomato sauce

3 medium carrots, thinly sliced (about 1 1/2 cups)

2 small onions, thinly sliced and separated into rings

2 cloves garlic, finely chopped

1/2 cup dry red wine or beef broth

2 tablespoons packed brown sugar

2 tablespoons chopped fresh or 1 1/2 teaspoons dried thyme leaves

Heat oven to 375°. Mix all ingredients in ungreased 3-quart casserole. Cover and bake 50 to 60 minutes or until mixture is hot and bubbly and carrots are tender.

1 Serving		% Daily Value:	
Calories	340	Vitamin A	48%
Calories from fat	35	Vitamin C	10%
Fat, g	4	Calcium	14%
Saturated, g	1	Iron	36%
Cholesterol, mg	25		
Sodium, mg	920		
Carbohydrate, g	61		
Dietary Fiber, g	13		
Protein, g	28		

Cajun Pork Chop Skillet

4 SERVINGS

▼

4 pork boneless loin or center cut chops, 3/4 inch thick (about 1 pound)

2 teaspoons Creole or Cajun seasoning

2 cups water

1 cup uncooked regular long-grain white rice

1 can (15 ounces) black beans, rinsed and drained

1 cup frozen green peas

Spray each side of pork chops with nonstick cooking spray. Rub Cajun seasoning over each side of pork. Spray 10-inch nonstick skillet with nonstick cooking spray; heat over medium-high heat. Cook pork chops in skillet until brown on both sides.

Stir in water and rice. Heat to boiling; reduce heat. Cover and simmer about 20 minutes or until liquid is absorbed and rice is tender. Stir in beans and peas. Cook about 5 minutes or until hot. Garnish with tomato wedges if desired.

1 Serving		% Daily Value:	
Calories	445	Vitamin A	2%
Calories from fat	70	Vitamin C	4%
Fat, g	8	Calcium	10%
Saturated, g	3	Iron	30%
Cholesterol, mg	55		
Sodium, mg	320		
Carbohydrate, g	70		
Dietary Fiber, g	10		
Protein, g	33		

Mexican Steak Stir-fry

4 SERVINGS

▤ ▼

Select the heat level you prefer by choosing mild, medium or hot salsa.

3/4 pound beef boneless sirloin, cut into 1 × 1/2-inch pieces

1 medium onion, chopped (about 1/2 cup)

1 small green bell pepper, chopped (about 1/2 cup)

1 clove garlic, finely chopped

1 cup frozen whole kernel corn

1/2 cup salsa

1 medium zucchini, sliced (about 2 cups)

1 can (15 to 16 ounces) pinto beans, rinsed and drained

1 can (14 1/2 ounces) no-salt-added whole tomatoes, undrained

Spray 12-inch nonstick skillet with nonstick cooking spray; heat over medium-high heat. Cook beef, onion, bell pepper and garlic in skillet 4 to 5 minutes, stirring frequently, until beef is no longer pink.

Stir in remaining ingredients, breaking up tomatoes. Cook about 5 minutes, stirring occasionally, until zucchini is tender and mixture is hot. Serve over hot cooked rice if desired.

1 Serving		% Daily Value:	
Calories	290	Vitamin A	26%
Calories from fat	35	Vitamin C	38%
Fat, g	1	Calcium	10%
Saturated, g	4	Iron	30%
Cholesterol, mg	40		
Sodium, mg	510		
Carbohydrate, g	47		
Dietary Fiber, g	12		
Protein, g	28		

Hearty Shepherd's Pie

6 TO 8 SERVINGS

Eggplant adds a new twist to this updated favorite.

1/2 pound extra-lean ground beef

1 large onion, chopped (about 1 cup)

1 clove garlic, finely chopped

1 medium eggplant (about 12 ounces), cut into 1/2-inch cubes (about 3 cups)

1 package (16 ounces) frozen broccoli, cauliflower and carrots

1 can (15 to 16 ounces) great northern beans, rinsed and drained

1 can (14 1/2 ounces) no-salt-added whole tomatoes, undrained

2 teaspoons Italian seasoning

1/2 teaspoon salt

1/4 teaspoon pepper

2 tablespoons water

2 tablespoons all-purpose flour

4 cups hot mashed potatoes

Heat oven to 350°. Spray rectangular baking dish, 13 × 9 × 2 inches, with nonstick cooking spray. Cook ground beef, onion and garlic in 12-inch nonstick skillet over medium heat, stirring occasionally, until beef is brown and onion is tender; drain. Stir in remaining ingredients except water, flour and potatoes, breaking up tomatoes. Heat to boiling; reduce heat. Simmer uncovered 15 minutes, stirring occasionally.

Shake water and flour in tightly covered container; stir into beef mixture. Spoon beef mixture into baking dish. Spoon potatoes evenly over beef mixture; spread to edges of dish. Bake uncovered about 30 minutes or until heated through. Let stand 5 minutes before serving.

1 Serving		% Daily Value:	
Calories	395	Vitamin A	68%
Calories from fat	115	Vitamin C	34%
Fat, g	13	Calcium	16%
Saturated, g	4	Iron	30%
Cholesterol, mg	25		
Sodium, mg	670		
Carbohydrate, g	60		
Dietary Fiber, g	11		
Protein, g	20		

BEAN ARITHMETIC

Dried legumes double to triple in volume as they cook, so be sure to use a sufficiently large pan or casserole. When purchasing or cooking dried legumes, use the following measurement chart as a guideline.

- 1 cup dried beans equals 8 ounces
- 1 cup dried beans equals 2 to 3 cups cooked beans
- 1 pound dried beans equals 6 cups cooked beans
- 1 can (15 to 16 ounce) beans, rinsed and drained equals 1 1/2 to 2 cups

Calypso Shrimp

4 SERVINGS

This citrus-spiked bean salsa is the perfect counter-point to the marinated shrimp.

Bean Salsa (below)

1/2 teaspoon grated orange peel

1 tablespoon orange juice

1 tablespoon vegetable oil

1 1/2 teaspoons chopped fresh or
    1/2 teaspoon dried thyme leaves

1 clove garlic, finely chopped

3/4 pound raw medium shrimp, peeled and
    deveined

Prepare Bean Salsa; set aside. Mix remaining ingredients except shrimp in medium bowl. Stir in shrimp. Spray 10-inch nonstick skillet with nonstick cooking spray; heat over medium-high heat. Cook shrimp mixture in skillet, turning shrimp once, until pink. Divide salsa among 4 serving plates. Arrange shrimp on salsa.

Bean Salsa

1 can (15 ounces) black beans, rinsed and
    drained

1 medium mango, peeled and chopped
    (about 1 cup)

1 small red bell pepper, chopped (about
    1/2 cup)

1/4 cup sliced green onions (2 to 3 medium)

1/2 teaspoon grated orange peel

2 tablespoons orange juice

1 tablespoon red wine vinegar

Mix all ingredients.

1 Serving		% Daily Value:	
Calories	235	Vitamin A	30%
Calories from fat	45	Vitamin C	36%
Fat, g	5	Calcium	10%
Saturated, g	1	Iron	22%
Cholesterol, mg	80		
Sodium, mg	350		
Carbohydrate, g	39		
Dietary Fiber, g	9		
Protein, g	18		

Lentil and Bulgur Burgers

10 SANDWICHES

Burgers aren't made just from hamburger anymore. These vegetarian burgers are filling and taste great!

2 cups dried lentils (1 pound), sorted and rinsed

6 cups water

1 bay leaf

2 cups water

1 cup uncooked bulgur or cracked wheat

1 cup soft whole wheat bread crumbs

1/3 cup low-sodium ketchup

1/4 cup cholesterol-free egg product or 2 egg whites

1/2 teaspoon celery salt

1/2 teaspoon ground mustard

1/4 teaspoon pepper

1 medium onion, finely chopped (about 1/2 cup)

1 clove garlic, finely chopped

10 whole wheat sandwich buns, split

Heat lentils, 6 cups water and the bay leaf to boiling in 8-quart saucepan; reduce heat. Cover and simmer about 45 minutes or until lentils are tender and water is absorbed.

Meanwhile, heat 2 cups water to boiling in 2-quart saucepan; remove from heat. Stir in bulgur. Cover and let stand 30 to 60 minutes or until water is absorbed.

Heat oven to 350°. Spray jelly roll pan, 15 1/2 × 10 1/2 × 1 inch, with nonstick cooking spray. Remove bay leaf from lentils. Thoroughly mix lentils, bulgur and remaining ingredients except buns in large bowl, using hands. Shape lentil mixture into ten 4-inch patties. Place in pan. Bake uncovered about 30 minutes, turning once, until firm but not dry. Serve on buns.

1 Serving		% Daily Value:	
Calories	285	Vitamin A	0%
Calories from fat	20	Vitamin C	2%
Fat, g	2	Calcium	8%
Saturated, g	1	Iron	30%
Cholesterol, mg	2		
Sodium, mg	360		
Carbohydrate, g	61		
Dietary Fiber, g	11		
Protein, g	17		

Soft Shell Tacos

10 TACOS

1/2 pound extra-lean ground beef

1 can (15 to 16 ounces) kidney beans, rinsed and drained

1 can (11 ounces) whole kernel corn with red and green peppers, drained

1 can (14 1/2 ounces) Mexican-style stewed tomatoes, undrained

10 nonfat flour tortillas (8 inches in diameter)

1 cup shredded carrots (about 1 1/2 medium)

1 cup shredded jicama

Cook ground beef in 10-inch nonstick skillet over medium-high heat, stirring occasionally, until brown; drain. Stir in beans, corn and tomatoes, breaking up tomatoes. Cook, stirring occasionally, until hot.

Spoon about 1/2 cup bean mixture onto each tortilla. Top each with about 2 tablespoons carrots and jicama; roll up. Serve with salsa and nonfat sour cream if desired.

1 Serving		% Daily Value:	
Calories	220	Vitamin A	20%
Calories from fat	25	Vitamin C	10%
Fat, g	3	Calcium	6%
Saturated, g	1	Iron	20%
Cholesterol, mg	15		
Sodium, mg	420		
Carbohydrate, g	42		
Dietary Fiber, g	6		
Protein, g	12		

WHAT IS A COMPLETE PROTEIN?

Protein for Life

Meatless foods can provide the adequate protein that we need for growth and maintenance of body tissues. Proteins are made of building blocks called amino acids. The body produces some of these amino acids, but those that it cannot produce, called *essential amino acids,* must come directly from the foods we eat. *Complete* or *high-quality* proteins, which contain all of the essential amino acids, come from animal sources such as meats, eggs, chicken, fish and dairy products. Nonanimal protein sources such as legumes, grains, pasta, cereals and breads, and nuts and seeds are *incomplete* or *lower-quality* proteins because they are missing at least one of the essential amino acid building blocks.

Complementing Combinations

To ensure we eat good quality protein, we can combine low-quality proteins. This way lesser-quality protein foods can *complement* or *complete* the amino acids missing from one another to create complete protein with equal quality to animal protein. Grains complement legumes; legumes complement nuts or seeds. The pairings are almost endless.

Familiar examples of high-quality protein include peanut butter on whole-wheat bread or a bean burrito (beans in a corn tortilla). By eating a low-quality protein food, such as pasta, with a high-quality protein, such as cheese, you can complete the protein as well.

Complementary protein foods do not have to be eaten in the same mouthful for you to reap the benefits of complete protein! Recent studies show that as long as you eat a variety of foods each day, you'll most likely eat enough complete protein to meet your needs. Learning how to complete protein sources is of great importance for vegetarians and for people in cultures who do not eat animal foods. However, for most of us who eat a varied daily diet, protein completion is generally not a problem.

Bean Basics

Collectively known as legumes because they come from leguminous plants (which produce pods with one row of seeds), beans, peas and lentils have been a staple food in cuisines throughout the world for thousands of years. Archeologists have discovered beans in ancient Egyptian tombs and in ruins of Native American habitats in the southwestern United States. The mild flavor of beans makes them perfect partners with spices and herbs. Extremely versatile, beans are used in appetizers, soups, salads, side dishes, sandwiches, main dishes and pizza. In some cuisines, beans are even used in desserts.

Beans are a powerhouse of nutrition. Abundant with soluble fiber, they combine well with grains, especially corn, wheat and rice, to create a complete protein. Beans are also virtually fat free, have no cholesterol and are a good source of vitamins. The bean recipes in this book use canned beans for ease and convenience, but any of the recipes can be made using dried beans. Directions for cooking dried legumes can found on page 148.

Bean Glossary

Adzuki Beans: Are small, oval, reddish-brown beans originating in China and Japan and have a light, nutty flavor. In Japan, the beans are steamed with rice, imparting a pink blush to the rice, and are served as a festival wedding dish.

Anasazi Beans: Are maroon spotted, white kidney-shaped beans. The Navajo word *Anasazi* means "ancient ones." Native Americans still grow these beans in the Southwest. Pinto beans make a nice substitute when Anasazi beans are unavailable.

Black Beans: Also called turtle beans, black beans are found in the cuisines of South and Central America as well as the Caribbean. They can be found canned and dried.

Black-eyed Peas: Also called blackeyes, black-eyed suzies or cowpeas, they are cream-colored with a small, dark brown to black spot on one end. Although native to China, black-eyed peas found their way to Africa and then to the southern United States. Black-eyed peas are used in the classic southern dish called Hoppin' John.

Butter Beans: Are large cream-colored lima beans. They can be found both canned and dried. Often served as a vegetable side dish, they can be added to soups, main dishes and salads.

Canellini Beans: Are large white kidney beans. Originally from South America, they have been adopted by Italians and are often mixed with pasta. Look for them with other canned beans.

Cranberry Beans: Also called Roman, shell or shellout beans, they are often used in Italian cooking. The beans are light pink in color with beige mottling, but their pink color is lost during cooking. Pinto beans can be substituted.

Fava Beans: Are large, flat beans that look brown and wrinkly when dried. Sometimes available fresh or canned in ethnic food stores, they have an earthy flavor and are the bean of choice for the Middle Eastern specialty falafel.

Garbanzo Beans: Also called chick-peas, are tan, bumpy and round, with a firm texture and mild nutty flavor. They are a good addition to soups, stews, casseroles and salads. Garbanzo beans are used in hummus, a popular Middle Eastern dip. They are available both canned and dried.

Great Northern Beans: Are white kidney-shaped beans. They are traditionally used in making baked beans and bean soup, and are commonly available canned and dried.

Kidney Beans: Are widely available both canned and dried in dark and light red. Used to add color and texture to many dishes, they are popular in chili and in red beans and rice.

Lentils: Are truly an ancient food, known to have been eaten in southwestern Asia around 7000 B.C. The familiar small greyish-green lentil is only one of the many types and colors of lentils used around the world. Lentils do not require soaking and cook in a relatively short time.

Lima Beans: Are available in 3 sizes: large, regular and baby. Limas are occasionally available fresh, otherwise they can be found frozen and dried (see also **Butter Beans**).

Mung Beans: Also known as grams or when hulled, moong dal. This sweet-flavored bean is native to India and spread to China where it is extremely popular. Americans know this bean in its sprouted form, either as fresh or canned bean sprouts.

Navy Beans: So called because they fed many a sailor in the early 1800s, they are white beans available canned and dried. Navy beans are also known as pea beans. Although smaller than cannellini and great northern beans, they would make a good substitute for either bean.

Pinto Beans: Are two-tone kidney-shaped beans widely used in Central and South American cooking. They turn a uniform pink when cooked, and are used for the Mexican staple refried beans. They're readily available canned and dried.

Continues

Soybeans: Are not widely eaten in the United States, but much of the harvest is processed into oil. More familiar forms of soybeans include tofu and textured vegetable protein products.

Split Peas: Both green and yellow, are available dried. Used mostly in soups, split peas cook relatively quickly.

(From top, going left to right)

Row 1: Pinto, Lima, Lentil, Navy
Row 2: Green Split Pea, Red Kidney, Adzuki, Black Beans
Row 3: Garbanzo, Cannellini, Fava, Black-eyed Peas
Row 4: Anasazi, Great Northern, Mung, Soy Beans

Lentil and Brown Rice Casserole

6 TO **8** SERVINGS

3/4 cup dried lentils, sorted and rinsed

1/2 cup uncooked brown rice

2 cans (10 1/2 ounces each) low-sodium ready-to-serve chicken broth

1/4 teaspoon salt

1 cup shredded reduced-fat Cheddar cheese (4 ounces)

1 package (16 ounces) frozen cut green beans or broccoli cuts, thawed and drained

Heat oven to 375°. Mix lentils, brown rice, broth, salt and 3/4 cup of the cheese in 2-quart casserole. Cover and bake 1 hour. Stir in green beans. Cover and bake about 30 minutes or until liquid is absorbed and rice is tender. Sprinkle with remaining 1/4 cup cheese.

1 Serving		% Daily Value:	
Calories	190	Vitamin A	6%
Calories from fat	35	Vitamin C	4%
Fat, g	4	Calcium	18%
Saturated, g	2	Iron	18%
Cholesterol, mg	10		
Sodium, mg	380		
Carbohydrate, g	31		
Dietary Fiber, g	7		
Protein, g	14		

Black Bean Cakes

4 SERVINGS

2 cans (15 ounces each) black beans, rinsed and drained

1/4 cup chopped fresh cilantro

1/4 cup sliced green onions (2 to 3 medium)

1 teaspoon chili powder

1 teaspoon chopped fresh or 1/4 teaspoon dried oregano leaves

1/4 teaspoon ground cumin

1 egg white, slightly beaten, or 2 tablespoons cholesterol-free egg product

1/2 cup frozen whole kernel corn, thawed

1/4 cup thick and chunky salsa

1/4 cup nonfat sour cream

2 tablespoons chopped fresh cilantro

Place beans in large bowl and mash. Stir in 1/4 cup cilantro, the onions, chili powder, oregano, cumin and egg white until well blended. Shape bean mixture into 4 patties, 1/2 inch thick. Spray both sides of each patty with nonstick cooking spray.

Spray 10-inch nonstick skillet with nonstick cooking spray; heat over medium-high heat. Cook patties in skillet about 6 minutes or until golden brown on both sides. Meanwhile, mix corn and salsa. Top each pattie with salsa mixture and garnish with sour cream and 2 tablespoons cilantro.

1 Serving		% Daily Value:	
Calories	322	Vitamin A	44%
Calories from fat	20	Vitamin C	26%
Fat, g	2	Calcium	20%
Saturated, g	0	Iron	36%
Cholesterol, mg	5		
Sodium, mg	880		
Carbohydrate, g	72		
Dietary Fiber, g	19		
Protein, g	23		

Bean L.T. Sandwiches

6 SANDWICHES

1 can (15 to 16 ounces) great northern, cannellini or navy beans, rinsed and drained

2/3 cup chopped red onion (about 1 small)

1/2 cup canned 1/3-less-salt clear chicken broth

1 1/2 teaspoons chopped fresh or 1/2 teaspoon dried thyme leaves

1/4 teaspoon salt

2 cloves garlic, finely chopped

6 whole wheat buns, split

6 slices tomato

3 cups shredded lettuce

Cook beans, onion, broth, thyme, salt and garlic in 2-quart saucepan over medium heat 6 to 8 minutes, stirring occasionally, until onion is tender. Place bean mixture in blender or food processor. Cover and blend until chunky. Cover and refrigerate 4 hours to blend flavors.

Spoon bean mixture onto bottom halves of buns. Top with tomato, lettuce and tops of buns.

1 Serving		% Daily Value:	
Calories	175	Vitamin A	2%
Calories from fat	10	Vitamin C	8%
Fat, g	1	Calcium	10%
Saturated, g	0	Iron	22%
Cholesterol, mg	0		
Sodium, mg	490		
Carbohydrate, g	37		
Dietary Fiber, g	6		
Protein, g	11		

Garbanzo Bean Sandwiches

4 SERVINGS, 8 SANDWICHES

Walnuts and garbanzo beans are a delicious duo in these hearty pita sandwiches.

1 can (15 to 16 ounces) garbanzo beans, rinsed and drained

1/2 cup water

2 tablespoons chopped fresh parsley

2 tablespoons chopped walnuts

1 tablespoon finely chopped onion

1 clove garlic, finely chopped

4 whole wheat pita breads (6 inches in diameter)

Lettuce leaves

1 medium tomato, seeded and chopped

1/2 medium cucumber, sliced and quartered

1/2 cup reduced-fat cucumber-ranch dressing

Place beans, water, parsley, walnuts, onion and garlic in food processor or blender. Cover and process until smooth. Cut each pita bread in half to form 2 pockets; line with lettuce leaves. Spoon 2 tablespoons bean spread into each pita half. Add tomato, cucumber and dressing.

1 Serving		% Daily Value:	
Calories	380	Vitamin A	6%
Calories from fat	90	Vitamin C	20%
Fat, g	10	Calcium	12%
Saturated, g	2	Iron	28%
Cholesterol, mg	0		
Sodium, mg	1040		
Carbohydrate, g	66		
Dietary Fiber, g	11		
Protein, g	17		

Garbanzo Bean Sandwiches

Bean Spaghetti

8 SERVINGS

Beans provide a protein punch in this meatless pasta favorite.

1 package (16 ounces) spaghetti

1 1/2 cups sliced mushrooms (about 4 ounces)

1 medium onion, chopped (about 1/2 cup)

1 small green bell pepper, chopped (about 1/2 cup)

1 jar (26 ounces) reduced-sodium spaghetti sauce

1 can (15 to 16 ounces) cannellini or great northern beans, rinsed and drained

1 can (15 to 16 ounces) kidney beans, rinsed and drained

1 can (14 1/2 ounces) no-salt-added whole tomatoes, drained

1 can (8 ounces) no-salt-added tomato sauce

1 can (6 ounces) no-salt-added tomato paste

Cook and drain spaghetti as directed on package. While spaghetti is cooking, spray 12-inch nonstick skillet with nonstick cooking spray; heat over medium-high heat. Cook mushrooms, onion and bell pepper in skillet about 5 minutes, stirring frequently, until vegetables are crisp-tender.

Stir in remaining ingredients, breaking up tomatoes. Heat to boiling, reduce heat. Simmer uncovered 10 to 15 minutes. Serve over spaghetti.

1 Serving		% Daily Value:	
Calories	450	Vitamin A	26%
Calories from fat	55	Vitamin C	40%
Fat, g	6	Calcium	14%
Saturated, g	1	Iron	44%
Cholesterol, mg	0		
Sodium, mg	320		
Carbohydrate, g	91		
Dietary Fiber, g	13		
Protein, g	21		

Black Bean Pita Pizzas

4 SERVINGS

4 whole wheat pita breads (4 inches in diameter)

1 medium onion, chopped (about 1/2 cup)

1 small green bell pepper, chopped (about 1/2 cup)

1 can (8 ounces) no-salt-added tomato sauce

1 can (15 ounces) black beans, rinsed and drained

1 teaspoon chili powder

1 teaspoon chopped fresh or 1/4 teaspoon dried oregano leaves

1/4 teaspoon ground cumin

3/4 cup shredded nonfat Cheddar cheese (3 ounces)

3/4 cup shredded nonfat Monterey Jack cheese (3 ounces)

1/2 cup nonfat sour cream

Heat oven to 425°. Split each pita bread in half around edge with knife. Place in ungreased jelly roll pan, 15 1/2 × 10 1/2 × 1 inch. Bake about 5 minutes or just until crisp.

Cook onion and bell pepper in tomato sauce in 10-inch nonstick skillet over medium heat about 5 minutes, stirring occasionally, until vegetables are crisp-tender. Stir in beans, chili powder, oregano and cumin; heat through.

Spoon bean mixture evenly over each pita bread half. Sprinkle evenly with cheeses. Bake 5 to 7 minutes or until cheeses are melted. Top each pizza with dollop of sour cream.

1 Serving		% Daily Value:	
Calories	315	Vitamin A	20%
Calories from fat	10	Vitamin C	16%
Fat, g	1	Calcium	46%
Saturated, g	0	Iron	24%
Cholesterol, mg	2		
Sodium, mg	610		
Carbohydrate, g	58		
Dietary Fiber, g	11		
Protein, g	29		

REDUCING FLATULENCE

Flatulence (intestinal gas) can result from eating beans. Gas is caused by the digestive system's inability to digest the complex sugars found in beans. This is lessened by draining the soaking liquid used to hydrate dried beans or by rinsing and draining canned beans. Minimal nutrition is lost by draining dried or canned beans. Additionally, over-the-counter products are available to help minimize this effect.

When incorporating more legumes into your diet, it is recommended that you add them gradually over a period of several weeks to allow your digestive system time to adjust. Sudden consumption of large amounts of legumes can cause bloating and gas.

Black Bean Lasagne

8 SERVINGS

Be prepared for rave reviews when you serve this lasagne. You may want to have a copy of the recipe ready for requests!

9 uncooked lasagne noodles

1 tablespoon vegetable oil

1 medium onion, chopped (about 1/2 cup)

1 clove garlic, finely chopped

1 cup water

2 tablespoons chopped fresh cilantro

2 cans (15 ounces each) black beans, rinsed and drained

1 can (14 1/2 ounces) no-salt-added whole tomatoes, undrained

2 cans (6 ounces each) no-salt-added tomato paste

1 container (15 ounces) nonfat ricotta cheese

1/2 cup reduced-fat grated Parmesan-style cheese (2 ounces)

1/2 cup cholesterol-free egg product or 4 egg whites

1/4 cup chopped fresh parsley

2 cups shredded reduced-fat Monterey Jack cheese (8 ounces)

Cook and drain noodles as directed on package. Rinse with hot water; drain. Heat oil in 12-inch nonstick skillet over medium-high heat. Cook onion and garlic in oil, stirring frequently, until onion is tender. Stir in water, cilantro, beans, tomatoes and tomato paste, breaking up tomatoes. Simmer uncovered 15 minutes, stirring occasionally. Mix remaining ingredients except Monterey Jack cheese.

Heat oven to 350°. Layer 1/3 each of the noodles, bean mixture, ricotta mixture and Monterey Jack cheese in ungreased rectangular baking dish, 13 × 9 × 2 inches. Repeat layers twice. Bake uncovered 30 to 35 minutes or until hot and bubbly. Let stand 10 to 15 minutes before cutting.

1 Serving		% Daily Value:	
Calories	410	Vitamin A	24%
Calories from fat	70	Vitamin C	26%
Fat, g	8	Calcium	54%
Saturated, g	2	Iron	32%
Cholesterol, mg	25		
Sodium, mg	710		
Carbohydrate, g	62		
Dietary Fiber, g	11		
Protein, g	34		

Curried Lentils and Rice

6 SERVINGS

1 cup dried lentils, sorted and rinsed

3 1/2 cups water

1 teaspoon curry powder

1/2 teaspoon salt

1/4 teaspoon pepper

1 large onion, chopped (about 1 cup)

1 clove garlic, finely chopped

1/2 cup uncooked regular long-grain white rice

1/2 cup plain nonfat or low-fat yogurt

1 large tomato, seeded and chopped (about 1 cup)

1/4 cup chopped fresh parsley

Mix lentils, water, curry powder, salt, pepper, onion and garlic in 2-quart saucepan. Heat to boiling; reduce heat. Cover and simmer 10 minutes. Stir in rice. Heat to boiling; reduce heat. Cover and simmer 25 to 28 minutes or until liquid is absorbed and rice is tender.

Mix yogurt, tomato and parsley. Serve over lentil mixture.

1 Serving		% Daily Value:	
Calories	175	Vitamin A	2%
Calories from fat	10	Vitamin C	8%
Fat, g	1	Calcium	6%
Saturated, g	0	Iron	22%
Cholesterol, mg	0		
Sodium, mg	200		
Carbohydrate, g	36		
Dietary Fiber, g	6		
Protein, g	11		

Moroccan Vegetables

5 SERVINGS

2 teaspoons vegetable oil

2 medium carrots, sliced (about 1 cup)

1 large onion, chopped (about 1 cup)

1 large red bell pepper, cut into 3/4-inch pieces (about 1 cup)

2 cloves garlic, finely chopped

1/2 cup raisins

1 teaspoon ground cumin

1/2 teaspoon salt

1/4 teaspoon ground turmeric

1/4 teaspoon ground cinnamon

1/8 teaspoon pepper

1 small zucchini, sliced (about 1 cup)

1 can (15 to 16 ounces) garbanzo beans, rinsed and drained

2 tablespoons chopped fresh parsley

Heat oil in 12-inch nonstick skillet over medium-high heat. Cook carrots, onion, bell pepper and garlic in oil about 4 minutes, stirring frequently, until onion is tender.

Stir in remaining ingredients except parsley. Cook about 5 minutes, stirring frequently, until zucchini is tender. Serve topped with parsley.

1 Serving		% Daily Value:	
Calories	220	Vitamin A	58%
Calories from fat	35	Vitamin C	40%
Fat, g	4	Calcium	8%
Saturated, g	1	Iron	20%
Cholesterol, mg	0		
Sodium, mg	440		
Carbohydrate, g	44		
Dietary Fiber, g	7		
Protein, g	9		

Moroccan Vegetables

Selection, Storage, Preparation and Cooking

Legume Primer

Selection

Many legume varieties are widely available in supermarkets. Specialty legumes may be found in the health food section of large supermarkets, in co-ops and health food stores or in specialty food mail-order catalogs. Many of these legumes are sold in bulk form.

- When purchasing legumes, bright uniform color and smooth, unbroken seed coats indicate quality and freshness.

- Legumes of the same size will result in even cooking.

- Sort before cooking to remove any damaged legumes or foreign matter.

Storage

Dried Legumes: Most legumes can be stored indefinitely, but for optimum quality and flavor, a 1- to 2-year storage time is recommended.

- Store in original packaging or transfer to airtight glass or plastic containers and label contents with starting storage date.

- Store in a cool (60° or less), dry location.

Cooked Legumes:

Refrigerator: Cooked legumes can be covered and stored in the refrigerator for up to 5 days.

Freezer: Cooked legumes can be frozen in airtight containers for up to 6 months.

Preparation

Soaking legumes before cooking helps to hydrate them and shortens the cooking time. Follow one of the soaking methods below:

Soaking Legumes: Recent findings indicate that all legumes, except lentils, need to be boiled uncovered 2 minutes before cooking to destroy an enzyme that can cause some people to become ill. This boiling time eliminates the need for the traditional long-soaking method to help rehydrate legumes. Although soaking for 8 to 24 hours is not necessary, it does allow for more uniform swelling of legumes.

If you choose to soak legumes before cooking, use one of the following methods:

Long-Soak Method: Place legumes in large saucepan or bowl in enough cold water to cover. Let stand at least 8 hours or overnight. Drain and rinse. Boil beans 2 minutes in enough water to cover; drain.

Quick-Soak Method: Boil beans 2 minutes in enough water to cover. Remove from heat; cover and let stand 1 hour before cooking; drain.

Cooking Tips

Cooking legumes in a microwave oven is not recommended due to the amount of liquid necessary to hydrate them and the long, slow cooking time required. Use of a pressure-cooker is also not recommended due to the foam created when cooking legumes. The foam can clog the pressure valve and may cause a sudden release of pressure, which could force the lid off without warning.

- Beans of similar size can easily be interchanged in recipes.
- Dried legumes double or triple in volume as they cook, so be sure to use a sufficiently large pan or casserole.
- To prevent beans from foaming when cooking, add 1 tablespoon margarine or vegetable oil to the cooking water; drain and rinse.
- Salt and acid tend to toughen beans. Add salt and acidic foods such as lemon juice, vinegar, tomatoes and tomato sauce, paste or juice only after the beans are soft, or the beans may not soften.
- High altitude and hard water may increase cooking times.
- Beans get drier with age and may take longer to cook. Very old beans may never soften completely.
- Simmer rather than boil beans and stir gently or the skins may burst.

LEGUME COOKING CHART

Legumes lose moisture with age, so you may find that you need more water than the recipe calls for. If all the water is absorbed but the legume isn't quite tender, add a little more water and cook longer. If it is tender but all the water hasn't been absorbed, drain if desired.

Type of Bean (1 cup dried amount)	Method of Cooking (using 3- to 4-quart saucepan with lid)	Approximate Cooking Time	Approximate Yield (in cups)
Adzuki	Add enough water to cover beans. Heat water and beans to a boil. Boil uncovered 2 minutes; reduce heat. Cover and simmer.	30 to 45 minutes	3
Anasazi, Black and Fava	Add enough water to cover beans. Heat water and beans to a boil. Boil uncovered 2 minutes; reduce heat. Cover and simmer.	1 to 2 hours	2
Black-eyed Peas, Butter, Canellini and Pinto	Add enough water to cover beans. Heat water and beans to a boil. Boil uncovered 2 minutes; reduce heat. Cover and simmer.	1 to 1 1/2 hours	2 to 2 1/2
Garbanzo	Add enough water to cover beans. Heat water and beans to a boil. Boil uncovered 2 minutes; reduce heat. Cover and simmer.	2 to 2 1/2 hours	2

Type of Bean (1 cup dried amount)	Method of Cooking (using 3- to 4-quart saucepan)	Approximate Cooking Time	Approximate Yield (in cups)
Great Northern	Add enough water to cover beans. Heat water and beans to a boil. Boil uncovered 2 minutes; reduce heat. Cover and simmer.	1 to 1 1/2 hours	2 to 3
Kidney	Add enough water to cover beans. Heat water and beans to a boil. Boil uncovered 2 minutes; reduce heat. Cover and simmer.	1 to 2 hours	2 to 2 1/2
Lentils	Add enough water to cover lentils. Heat water and lentils to a boil. Reduce heat. Cover and simmer.	30 to 45 minutes	2 to 2 1/4
Lima and Navy	Add enough water to cover beans. Heat water and beans to a boil. Boil uncovered 2 minutes; reduce heat. Cover and simmer.	1 to 1 1/2 hours	2
Mung	Add enough water to cover beans. Heat water and beans to a boil. Boil uncovered 2 minutes; reduce heat. Cover and simmer.	45 to 60 minutes	2

LEGUME COOKING CHART *(Continued)*

Type of Bean (1 cup dried amount)	Method of Cooking (using 3- to 4-quart saucepan)	Approximate Cooking Time	Approximate Yield (in cups)
Soy	Add enough water to cover beans. Heat water and beans to a boil. Boil uncovered 2 minutes; reduce heat. Cover and simmer.	3 to 4 hours	2
Split Peas	Add enough water to cover split peas. Heat water and split peas to a boil. Boil uncovered 2 minutes; reduce heat. Cover and simmer.	45 to 60	2 1/4

Cuban Black Beans and Rice

6 SERVINGS

1 large onion, chopped (about 1 cup)

1 medium green bell pepper, chopped (about 1 cup)

1 large carrot, chopped (about 2/3 cup)

2 cloves garlic, finely chopped

1 cup orange juice

2 teaspoons paprika

1 teaspoon ground coriander

1/4 teaspoon salt

1/8 teaspoon crushed red pepper

1 can (14 1/2 ounces) no-salt-added whole tomatoes, undrained

1 can (15 ounces) black beans, rinsed and drained

4 cups hot cooked brown rice

1 cup plain nonfat yogurt

1 lime, cut into 6 wedges

Heat onion, bell pepper, carrot, garlic, orange juice, paprika, coriander, salt, red pepper and tomatoes to boiling in 2-quart saucepan, breaking up tomatoes; reduce heat. Cover and simmer about 45 minutes, stirring occasionally, until thick; remove from heat.

Stir beans into vegetable mixture. Place 1 cup of the bean mixture in blender or food processor. Cover and blend about 30 seconds or until smooth. Stir blended mixture into bean mixture in saucepan. Cook over medium heat about 3 minutes or until hot. Serve over rice with yogurt and lime wedges.

1 Serving		% Daily Value:	
Calories	290	Vitamin A	38%
Calories from fat	20	Vitamin C	36%
Fat, g	2	Calcium	18%
Saturated, g	1	Iron	18%
Cholesterol, mg	0		
Sodium, mg	670		
Carbohydrate, g	65		
Dietary Fiber, g	10		
Protein, g	13		

Sweet Potatoes and Black Beans

5 SERVINGS

The tastes of the Caribbean are found in this well-seasoned side dish.

3 sweet potatoes, peeled and cut into 3/4-inch cubes (about 3 cups)

3/4 cup orange juice

2 teaspoons cornstarch

1/2 teaspoon ground coriander

1/2 teaspoon ground allspice

1/2 teaspoon grated gingerroot or 1/4 teaspoon ground ginger

1/4 teaspoon ground cumin

1 can (15 ounces) black beans, rinsed and drained

1 cup cooked rice

Place sweet potatoes in 2-quart saucepan adding enough water just to cover sweet potatoes. Heat water and sweet potatoes to boiling; reduce heat. Cover and simmer 10 to 12 minutes or until tender; drain and set aside.

Mix remaining ingredients except beans and rice in same saucepan. Heat to boiling. Boil 1 minute or until thickened, stirring constantly. Stir in sweet potatoes, beans and rice. Cook about 2 minutes or until hot.

1 Serving		% Daily Value:	
Calories	225	Vitamin A	100%
Calories from fat	10	Vitamin C	26%
Fat, g	1	Calcium	8%
Saturated, g	0	Iron	16%
Cholesterol, mg	0		
Sodium, mg	330		
Carbohydrate, g	53		
Dietary Fiber, g	8		
Protein, g	9		

Cajun Side Dish

6 SERVINGS

When selecting okra, look for fresh pods that are bright green in color, firm and under 4 inches long.

1 tablespoon vegetable oil

2 1/2 cups sliced okra (about 8 ounces)

1 cup frozen whole kernel corn

1 large onion, chopped (about 1 cup)

1 medium green, red or yellow bell pepper, chopped (about 1 cup)

3 large tomatoes, seeded and chopped (about 3 cups)

1 can (15 to 16 ounces) black-eyed peas, rinsed and drained

2 teaspoons chopped fresh or 1/2 teaspoon dried thyme leaves

2 teaspoons chopped fresh or 1/2 teaspoon dried oregano leaves

1/2 teaspoon salt

1/2 teaspoon paprika

1/8 to 1/4 teaspoon ground red pepper (cayenne)

Heat oil in 12-inch nonstick skillet over medium-high heat. Cook okra, corn, onion and bell pepper in oil, stirring frequently, until crisp-tender. Stir in remaining ingredients. Cook about 5 minutes, stirring frequently, until hot.

1 Serving		% Daily Value:	
Calories	135	Vitamin A	10%
Calories from fat	25	Vitamin C	26%
Fat, g	3	Calcium	8%
Saturated, g	1	Iron	16%
Cholesterol, mg	0		
Sodium, mg	360		
Carbohydrate, g	30		
Dietary Fiber, g	11		
Protein, g	8		

Cajun Side Dish

Marinated Black-eyed Peas

8 SERVINGS

1/4 cup chopped red onion

2 medium stalks celery, chopped (about 1 cup)

1 small green bell pepper, chopped (about 1/2 cup)

1 jalapeño chile, chopped

2 cans (15 to 16 ounces each) black-eyed peas, rinsed and drained

2 tablespoons red wine vinegar

1 tablespoon olive or vegetable oil

1/4 teaspoon salt

1/8 teaspoon pepper

1 clove garlic, finely chopped

Mix onion, celery, bell pepper, chile and peas in large bowl. Mix remaining ingredients. Pour over pea mixture; toss. Cover and refrigerate at least 2 hours but no longer than 24 hours, stirring occasionally.

1 Serving		% Daily Value:	
Calories	100	Vitamin A	6%
Calories from fat	20	Vitamin C	30%
Fat, g	2	Calcium	4%
Saturated, g	0	Iron	16%
Cholesterol, mg	0		
Sodium, mg	340		
Carbohydrate, g	24		
Dietary Fiber, g	11		
Protein, g	8		

Sweet-and-Sour Veggies and Beans

4 SERVINGS

Using purchased sweet-and-sour sauce makes this recipe extra easy. Try serving it with grilled turkey burgers.

1/2 cup water

1 package (16 ounces) frozen broccoli, carrots, water chestnuts and red peppers

1 can (15 to 16 ounces) kidney beans, rinsed and drained

1/3 cup sweet-and-sour sauce

1 tablespoon sesame seed, toasted

Heat water to boiling in 12-inch nonstick skillet. Cook vegetables in water 4 to 6 minutes, stirring occasionally, until tender. Stir in beans and sweet-and-sour sauce; heat through, stirring occasionally. Sprinkle with sesame seed. Serve warm or cold.

1 Serving		% Daily Value:	
Calories	175	Vitamin A	78%
Calories from fat	20	Vitamin C	26%
Fat, g	2	Calcium	6%
Saturated, g	0	Iron	22%
Cholesterol, mg	0		
Sodium, mg	360		
Carbohydrate, g	38		
Dietary Fiber, g	11		
Protein, g	12		

Succotash Chicken Soup

10 SERVINGS

1/2 pound skinless, boneless chicken thighs, cut into 1/2-inch pieces

1 medium onion, chopped (about 1/2 cup)

1 small green bell pepper, chopped (about 1/2 cup)

1 clove garlic, finely chopped

1 cup frozen whole kernel corn

1/4 cup chopped fresh parsley

4 cups water

1 tablespoon low-sodium Worcestershire sauce

1 1/2 teaspoons chopped fresh or 1/2 teaspoon dried thyme leaves

1/4 teaspoon ground red pepper (cayenne)

1 can (15 to 16 ounces) butter beans, rinsed and drained

1 can (14 1/2 ounces) no-salt-added whole tomatoes, undrained

1 package (9 ounces) frozen lima beans

1/2 cup water

3 tablespoons all-purpose flour

Spray nonstick Dutch oven with nonstick cooking spray. Cook chicken, onion, bell pepper and garlic in Dutch oven over medium-high heat about 5 minutes, stirring occasionally, until chicken is no longer pink in center. Stir in remaining ingredients except 1/2 cup water and the flour, breaking up tomatoes. Heat to boiling.

Shake 1/2 cup water and the flour in tightly covered container. Gradually stir flour mixture into soup; reduce heat. Simmer uncovered until thickened.

1 Serving		% Daily Value:	
Calories	125	Vitamin A	4%
Calories from fat	20	Vitamin C	14%
Fat, g	2	Calcium	4%
Saturated, g	1	Iron	12%
Cholesterol, mg	15		
Sodium, mg	140		
Carbohydrate, g	22		
Dietary Fiber, g	2		
Protein, g	11		

Ratatouille Chile

7 SERVINGS

1/2 pound ground turkey breast

1 large eggplant (about 1 pound), cut into 1/2-inch cubes (about 4 cups)

1 large onion, chopped (about 1 cup)

1 medium green bell pepper, chopped (about 1 cup)

1 clove garlic, finely chopped

1/2 cup sliced zucchini

2 to 3 teaspoons chili powder

1 teaspoon chopped fresh or 1/4 teaspoon dried oregano leaves

1/4 teaspoon ground cumin

1/4 teaspoon salt

1 can (15 to 16 ounces) great northern beans, rinsed and drained

1 can (14 1/2 ounces) no-salt-added whole tomatoes, undrained

1 can (8 ounces) no-salt-added tomato sauce

Cook ground turkey, eggplant, onion, bell pepper and garlic in nonstick Dutch oven over medium-high heat about 10 minutes, stirring occasionally, until turkey is no longer pink and eggplant is tender; drain. Stir in remaining ingredients, breaking up tomatoes. Cook about 10 minutes, stirring occasionally, until zucchini is tender.

1 Serving		% Daily Value:	
Calories	165	Vitamin A	10%
Calories from fat	20	Vitamin C	22%
Fat, g	2	Calcium	8%
Saturated, g	1	Iron	20%
Cholesterol, mg	20		
Sodium, mg	270		
Carbohydrate, g	29		
Dietary Fiber, g	7		
Protein, g	15		

Split Pea–Wild Rice Soup

5 SERVINGS

2 cups dried green split peas (about 1 pound), rinsed and drained

9 cups water

1 tablespoon low-sodium chicken bouillon granules

3 medium carrots, coarsely chopped (about 1 1/2 cups)

1 large onion, coarsely chopped (about 1 cup)

2 cloves garlic, finely chopped

1 bay leaf

3/4 cup uncooked wild rice

1/2 pound fully cooked smoked reduced-sodium ham, cut into 1/4-inch pieces (about 1 cup)

Heat all ingredients except wild rice and ham to boiling in Dutch oven, stirring occasionally; reduce heat. Cover and simmer 1 hour.

Stir in wild rice and ham. Heat to boiling; reduce heat. Cover loosely and simmer about 1 hour or until desired consistency. Remove bay leaf.

1 Serving		% Daily Value:	
Calories	415	Vitamin A	66%
Calories from fat	25	Vitamin C	10%
Fat, g	3	Calcium	6%
Saturated, g	1	Iron	22%
Cholesterol, mg	15		
Sodium, mg	260		
Carbohydrate, g	78		
Dietary Fiber, g	10		
Protein, g	29		

Lentil, Barley and Kielbasa Soup

6 SERVINGS

This hearty soup would go well with multigrain bread or rolls and a crisp tossed salad.

1/2 pound fully cooked reduced-fat turkey kielbasa sausage, cut into 6 pieces

1 large onion, chopped (about 1 cup)

2 medium stalks celery, chopped (about 1 cup)

2 medium carrots, chopped (about 1 cup)

2 cloves garlic, finely chopped

3/4 cup dried lentils, sorted and rinsed

1/2 cup uncooked pearled barley

6 cups water

1 tablespoon low-sodium chicken bouillon granules

1 1/2 teaspoons chopped fresh or 1/2 teaspoon dried rosemary leaves, crushed

1 1/2 teaspoons chopped fresh or 1/2 teaspoon dried oregano leaves

1 bay leaf

1 can (28 ounces) no-salt-added whole tomatoes, undrained

1/4 cup chopped fresh parsley

Cook sausage, onion, celery, carrots and garlic in nonstick Dutch oven over medium heat about 8 minutes, stirring occasionally, until vegetables are tender. Stir in remaining ingredients except parsley, breaking up tomatoes. Heat to boiling; reduce heat to medium-low. Simmer uncovered about 45 minutes, stirring occasionally, until lentils are tender. Remove bay leaf. Stir in parsley.

1 Serving		% Daily Value:	
Calories	245	Vitamin A	46%
Calories from fat	45	Vitamin C	32%
Fat, g	5	Calcium	8%
Saturated, g	2	Iron	24%
Cholesterol, mg	15		
Sodium, mg	430		
Carbohydrate, g	44		
Dietary Fiber, g	9		
Protein, g	15		

Hearty Seafood Stew

7 SERVINGS

2 medium carrots, sliced (about 1 cup)

2 medium stalks celery, sliced (about 1 cup)

1 large onion, chopped (about 1 cup)

1 clove garlic, finely chopped

1 can (14 1/2 ounces) no-salt-added stewed tomatoes, undrained

2 cups water

2 teaspoons low-sodium beef bouillon granules

1 medium potato, cut into 1/2-inch pieces (about 1 cup)

1/2 pound catfish fillets, cut into 1-inch pieces

1/4 pound peeled and deveined raw medium shrimp

1 can (15 to 16 ounces) great northern beans, rinsed and drained

1 small zucchini, cut lengthwise in half and crosswise into slices (about 1 cup)

1 teaspoon chopped fresh or 1/4 teaspoon dried thyme leaves

Chopped fresh parsley, if desired

Spray nonstick Dutch oven with nonstick cooking spray; heat over medium-high heat. Cook carrots, celery, onion and garlic in Dutch oven, stirring frequently, until vegetables are tender. Stir in tomatoes, water, bouillon granules and potato. Heat to boiling; reduce heat. Cover and simmer 20 minutes, stirring occasionally.

Stir in catfish, shrimp, beans, zucchini and thyme. Heat to boiling; reduce heat. Cover and simmer about 10 minutes or until fish flakes easily with fork. Serve topped with parsley.

1 Serving		% Daily Value:	
Calories	155	Vitamin A	38%
Calories from fat	10	Vitamin C	14%
Fat, g	1	Calcium	10%
Saturated, g	0	Iron	20%
Cholesterol, mg	40		
Sodium, mg	230		
Carbohydrate, g	26		
Dietary Fiber, g	6		
Protein, g	16		

Hearty Seafood Stew

Barbecue Beef and Bean Stew

7 SERVINGS

Spray Dutch oven with nonstick cooking spray; heat over medium-high heat. Cook beef, onion, celery, bell pepper and garlic in Dutch oven, stirring occasionally, until beef is brown and vegetables are tender. Stir in 2 cups water and the bouillon granules. Heat to boiling; reduce heat. Cover and simmer 1 hour, stirring occasionally. Stir in beans and tomatoes, breaking up tomatoes. Shake 2 tablespoons water and the flour in tightly covered container; stir into stew. Heat to boiling. Boil, stirring frequently, until thickened.

1 pound beef stew meat, cut into 1/2-inch pieces

1 medium onion, coarsely chopped (about 1/2 cup)

1 medium stalk celery, chopped (about 1/2 cup)

1 small green bell pepper, chopped (about 1/2 cup)

1 clove garlic, finely chopped

2 cups water

2 teaspoons low-sodium beef bouillon granules

1 can (16 ounces) barbecue beans

1 can (15 to 16 ounces) butter beans, rinsed and drained

1 can (14 1/2 ounces) no-salt-added whole tomatoes, undrained

2 tablespoons water

2 tablespoons all-purpose flour

1 Serving		% Daily Value:	
Calories	210	Vitamin A	6%
Calories from fat	55	Vitamin C	18%
Fat, g	6	Calcium	6%
Saturated, g	2	Iron	22%
Cholesterol, mg	25		
Sodium, mg	370		
Carbohydrate, g	30		
Dietary Fiber, g	9		
Protein, g	18		

Navy Bean and Pasta Soup

8 SERVINGS

1 large onion, chopped (about 1 cup)

1 medium stalk celery, chopped (about 1/2 cup)

1 medium carrot, chopped (about 1/2 cup)

3 cans (14 1/2 ounces each) 1/3-less-salt clear chicken broth

2 cans (15 to 16 ounces each) navy beans, rinsed and drained

1 bay leaf

1 tablespoon chopped fresh or 1 teaspoon dried oregano leaves

1 cup uncooked ditalini pasta or small elbow macaroni

2 slices reduced-sodium bacon, cooked and crumbled

1/4 cup chopped fresh parsley

Cook onion, celery and carrot in 1/4 cup of the broth in nonstick Dutch oven, stirring occasionally, until onion is tender. Stir in remaining broth, the beans, bay leaf and oregano. Heat to boiling. Stir in pasta. Simmer 10 to 15 minutes or until pasta is tender. Remove bay leaf. Stir in bacon. Serve soup topped with parsley.

1 Serving		% Daily Value:	
Calories	210	Vitamin A	14%
Calories from fat	20	Vitamin C	4%
Fat, g	2	Calcium	10%
Saturated, g	1	Iron	20%
Cholesterol, mg	2		
Sodium, mg	550		
Carbohydrate, g	44		
Dietary Fiber, g	9		
Protein, g	13		

Italian Bean Salad

6 SERVINGS

This Italian classic is simple and tasty; it is a nice side dish for grilled meats.

1/3 cup sliced green onions (about 3 medium)

1/4 cup chopped fresh parsley

1/2 cup nonfat Italian dressing

2 medium tomatoes, seeded and chopped (about 1 1/2 cups)

1 can (15 to 16 ounces) cannellini or great northern beans, rinsed and drained

Mix all ingredients. Cover and refrigerate 1 to 2 hours to blend flavors.

1 Serving		% Daily Value:	
Calories	110	Vitamin A	4%
Calories from fat	20	Vitamin C	20%
Fat, g	2	Calcium	6%
Saturated, g	0	Iron	16%
Cholesterol, mg	0		
Sodium, mg	330		
Carbohydrate, g	21		
Dietary Fiber, g	5		
Protein, g	7		

Vegetarian Chili

7 SERVINGS

1/2 cup no-salt-added tomato juice

1/2 cup uncooked bulgur or cracked wheat

1 cup frozen whole kernel corn

1 1/2 teaspoons chili powder

1 teaspoon chopped fresh or 1/4 teaspoon dried oregano leaves

1/2 teaspoon ground cumin

1 large onion, chopped (about 1 cup)

1 small green bell pepper, chopped (about 1/2 cup)

2 cloves garlic, finely chopped

1 can (28 ounces) no-salt-added whole tomatoes, undrained

1 can (15 to 16 ounces) kidney beans, rinsed and drained

1 can (15 ounces) black beans, rinsed and drained

Heat tomato juice to boiling over high heat in 1-quart saucepan; remove from heat. Stir in bulgur. Cover and let stand 30 to 60 minutes or until juice is absorbed.

Mix remaining ingredients in nonstick Dutch oven, breaking up tomatoes. Cook over medium-high heat, stirring frequently, until vegetables are tender. Stir in bulgur; heat through. Serve topped with nonfat sour cream, shredded reduced-fat Cheddar cheese and chopped fresh cilantro if desired.

1 Serving		% Daily Value:	
Calories	215	Vitamin A	10%
Calories from fat	10	Vitamin C	24%
Fat, g	1	Calcium	10%
Saturated, g	0	Iron	26%
Cholesterol, mg	0		
Sodium, mg	320		
Carbohydrate, g	51		
Dietary Fiber, g	14		
Protein, g	14		

Southwestern Beef and Bean Stew

8 SERVINGS

Offer steaming hot cornbread or corn muffins along with this hearty stew.

1/4 cup all-purpose flour

1/2 teaspoon salt

1/4 teaspoon pepper

1 pound beef stew meat, cut into 1/2- to 3/4-inch cubes

1 tablespoon vegetable oil

1 large onion, chopped (about 1 cup)

1 small green bell pepper, chopped (about 1/2 cup)

2 cloves garlic, finely chopped

1 3/4 cups water

1 1/2 teaspoons low-sodium beef bouillon granules

1 teaspoon chili powder

1 teaspoon chopped fresh or 1/4 teaspoon dried oregano leaves

1/4 teaspoon ground cumin

1 can (14 1/2 ounces) no-salt-added whole tomatoes, drained

1 can (15 to 16 ounces) pinto beans, rinsed and drained

1 cup frozen whole kernel corn

Shake flour, salt and pepper in large plastic bag. Add beef; shake to coat with flour mixture. Heat oil in nonstick Dutch oven over medium-high heat. Cook beef, onion, bell pepper and garlic in oil, stirring occasionally, until beef is brown.

Stir in water, bouillon granules, chili powder, oregano and cumin. Heat to boiling; reduce heat. Cover and simmer 1 hour. Stir in tomatoes, beans and corn, breaking up tomatoes; heat through.

1 Serving		% Daily Value:	
Calories	200	Vitamin A	4%
Calories from fat	65	Vitamin C	12%
Fat, g	7	Calcium	4%
Saturated, g	2	Iron	16%
Cholesterol, mg	20		
Sodium, mg	290		
Carbohydrate, g	26		
Dietary Fiber, g	6		
Protein, g	14		

Thai Chicken Salad

4 SERVINGS

⧗ ⩔

Dressing (right)

3/4 pound skinless, boneless chicken breasts, cut into 2 × 1/4-inch strips

1/4 teaspoon garlic salt

1 package (16 ounces) frozen broccoli, carrots, water chestnuts and red peppers

2 tablespoons water

1 can (15 to 16 ounces) great northern beans, rinsed and drained

4 cups shredded savoy cabbage, red cabbage, bok choy or lettuce

1/3 cup sliced green onions (about 3 medium)

Prepare Dressing; set aside. Spray 10-inch nonstick skillet with nonstick cooking spray; heat over medium-high heat. Cook chicken in skillet 5 to 7 minutes, stirring occasionally, until no longer pink in center. Remove chicken from skillet; sprinkle chicken with garlic salt.

Spray skillet with nonstick cooking spray; heat over medium-high heat. Cook frozen vegetables and water in skillet 5 to 7 minutes, stirring frequently, until vegetables are crisp-tender. Stir in beans; heat through. Divide cabbage among 4 serving plates. Top with vegetable mixture, onions and chicken. Serve with Dressing. Serve salad warm or cold.

Dressing

1/2 cup water

2 tablespoons white wine vinegar

1 tablespoon low-sodium soy sauce

2 teaspoons honey

1 1/2 teaspoons cornstarch

1 tablespoon reduced-fat peanut butter

1 tablespoon chopped fresh cilantro

1/4 teaspoon crushed red pepper

1 clove garlic, finely chopped

Mix water, vinegar, soy sauce, honey and cornstarch in 1-quart saucepan. Heat to boiling. Boil, stirring constantly, until thickened and clear. Stir in remaining ingredients with wire whisk.

1 Serving		% Daily Value:	
Calories	310	Vitamin A	80%
Calories from fat	45	Vitamin C	46%
Fat, g	5	Calcium	18%
Saturated, g	1	Iron	34%
Cholesterol, mg	45		
Sodium, mg	690		
Carbohydrate, g	44		
Dietary Fiber, g	11		
Protein, g	33		

Turkey Taco Salads

4 SERVINGS

[I] [W]

3 flour tortillas (8 inches in diameter)

1/2 pound ground turkey breast

1/3 cup water

1 to 2 teaspoons chile powder

1/2 teaspoon salt

1/4 teaspoon garlic powder

1/4 teaspoon ground red pepper (cayenne)

1 can (8 ounces) kidney beans, drained

5 cups shredded lettuce

1 large tomato, chopped (about 1 cup)

1 small onion, chopped (about 1/4 cup)

1/2 cup shredded reduced-fat Monterey Jack cheese (2 ounces)

1/4 cup nonfat Thousand Island dressing

1/4 cup nonfat sour cream

4 pitted ripe olives, sliced

Heat oven to 400°. Cut tortillas into 12 wedges or strips, about 3 × 1/4 inch. Place in ungreased jelly roll pan, 15 1/2 × 10 1/2 × 1 inch. Bake 6 to 8 minutes, stirring at least once, until golden brown and crisp; cool.

Cook ground turkey in 10-inch nonstick skillet, stirring occasionally, until no longer pink; drain. Stir in water, chili powder, salt, garlic powder, red pepper and beans. Heat to boiling; reduce heat. Simmer uncovered 2 to 3 minutes, stirring occasionally, until liquid is absorbed. Cool 10 minutes.

Mix lettuce, tomato, onion and cheese in large bowl; toss with Thousand Island dressing. Divide lettuce mixture among 4 serving plates. Top each with about 1/2 cup turkey mixture. Arrange tortilla wedges around salads. Garnish with sour cream and olives.

1 Serving		% Daily Value:	
Calories	350	Vitamin A	12%
Calories from fat	90	Vitamin C	18%
Fat, g	10	Calcium	18%
Saturated, g	3	Iron	24%
Cholesterol, mg	60		
Sodium, mg	775		
Carbohydrate, g	41		
Dietary Fiber, g	7		
Protein, g	31		

Mediterranean Salad

8 SERVINGS

[I] [♥] [W]

2 medium oranges

2/3 cup finely chopped red bell pepper

1/2 cup shredded fresh spinach

2 tablespoons halved Kalamata or ripe olives

1 can (15 to 16 ounces) great northern or garbanzo beans, rinsed and drained

3 tablespoons red wine vinegar

2 tablespoons olive or vegetable oil

1/8 teaspoon pepper

1 clove garlic, finely chopped

Peel oranges and remove membrane; cut into 1-inch pieces. Mix oranges, bell pepper, spinach, olives and beans in medium bowl. Shake remaining ingredients in tightly covered container. Pour over orange mixture; toss.

1 Serving		% Daily Value:	
Calories	110	Vitamin A	8%
Calories from fat	35	Vitamin C	56%
Fat, g	4	Calcium	6%
Saturated, g	1	Iron	12%
Cholesterol, mg	0		
Sodium, mg	150		
Carbohydrate, g	18		
Dietary Fiber, g	4		
Protein, g	5		

Bean and Cabbage Slaw

5 SERVINGS

The pre-packaged, shredded cabbage and carrot mixture makes short work of coleslaw salads.

1/2 cup white vinegar

1/2 cup sugar

1/2 teaspoon salt

1 to 2 tablespoons chopped fresh or 1 to 2 teaspoons dried dill weed

4 cups coleslaw mix

1 can (15 to 16 ounces) black-eyed peas, garbanzo beans or black beans, rinsed and drained

Heat vinegar, sugar, salt and dill weed to boiling in 1-quart saucepan, stirring occasionally. Boil about 2 minutes, stirring occasionally, until sugar is dissolved.

Mix coleslaw mix and peas in large bowl. Pour vinegar mixture over coleslaw mixture; stir to mix well. Cover and refrigerate at least 4 hours but no longer than 24 hours. Drain before serving.

1 Serving		% Daily Value:	
Calories	175	Vitamin A	18%
Calories from fat	10	Vitamin C	28%
Fat, g	1	Calcium	4%
Saturated, g	0	Iron	14%
Cholesterol, mg	0		
Sodium, mg	430		
Carbohydrate, g	43		
Dietary Fiber, g	9		
Protein, g	7		

Oriental Pork Salad

4 SERVINGS

2 tablespoons low-sodium soy sauce

1 tablespoon chile puree with garlic

1 teaspoon vegetable oil

3/4 pound boneless pork tenderloin, cut into 1 1/2 × 1/2-inch strips

2 1/2 cups coleslaw mix

1 small red bell pepper, cut into 1/2-inch strips

1 can (15 ounces) black beans, rinsed and drained

Toasted sesame seed, if desired

Mix soy sauce, chile puree and oil. Mix pork and 1 tablespoon of the soy sauce mixture; reserve remaining soy sauce mixture. Spray 10-inch nonstick skillet with nonstick cooking spray; heat over medium-high heat. Cook pork in skillet, stirring occasionally, until no longer pink. Place pork in medium bowl. To serve, spoon pork mixture onto serving platter. Drizzle with remaining soy sauce mixture, sprinkle with sesame seed if desired.

1 Serving		% Daily Value:	
Calories	340	Vitamin A	28%
Calories from fat	100	Vitamin C	30%
Fat, g	11	Calcium	10%
Saturated, g	4	Iron	22%
Cholesterol, mg	70		
Sodium, mg	650		
Carbohydrate, g	34		
Dietary Fiber, g	9		
Protein, g	35		

Oriental Pork Salad

Nutrition Information

Nutrition Guidelines:

Daily Values are set by the Food and Drug Administration and are based on the needs of most healthy adults. Current nutrition labels of food packages use the term Daily Value instead of the term U.S. RDA (United States Recommended Daily Allowance), but the amounts remain the same. Percent Daily Values are based on an average diet of 2,000 calories per day. Your daily values may be higher or lower depending on your calorie needs.

Recommended intake for a daily diet of 2,000 calories:

Total Fat	Less than 65 g
Saturated Fat	Less than 20g
Cholesterol	Less than 300mg
Sodium	Less than 2,400mg
Total Carbohydrate	300g
Dietary Fiber	25g

Criteria Used for Calculating Nutrition Information:

- The first ingredient is used wherever a choice is given (such as 1/3 cup sour cream or plain yogurt).

- The first ingredient amount is used wherever a range is given (such as 2 to 3 teaspoons milk).

- The first serving number is used wherever a range is given (such as 4 to 6 servings).

- "If desired" ingredients are not included, whether mentioned in the ingredient list or in the recipe directions as a suggestion (such as, "Sprinkle with brown sugar if desired").

- Only the amount of a marinade or frying oil that is absorbed during preparation is calculated.

Metric Conversion Guide

Volume

U.S. Units	Canadian Metric	Australian Metric
1/4 teaspoon	1 mL	1 ml
1/2 teaspoon	2 mL	2 ml
1 teaspoon	5 mL	5 ml
1 tablespoon	15 mL	20 ml
1/4 cup	50 mL	60 ml
1/3 cup	75 mL	80 ml
1/2 cup	125 mL	125 ml
2/3 cup	150 mL	170 ml
3/4 cup	175 mL	190 ml
1 cup	250 mL	250 ml
1 quart	1 liter	1 liter
1 1/2 quarts	1.5 liters	1.5 liters
2 quarts	2 liters	2 liters
2 1/2 quarts	2.5 liters	2.5 liters
3 quarts	3 liters	3 liters
4 quarts	4 liters	4 liters

Weight

U.S. Units	Canadian Metric	Australian Metric
1 ounce	30 grams	30 grams
2 ounces	55 grams	60 grams
3 ounces	85 grams	90 grams
4 ounces (1/4 pound)	115 grams	125 grams
8 ounces (1/2 pound)	225 grams	225 grams
16 ounces (1 pound)	455 grams	500 grams
1 pound	455 grams	1/2 kilogram

Note: The recipes in this cookbook have not been developed or tested using metric measures. When converting recipes to metric, some variations in quality may be noted.

Measurements

Inches	Centimeters
1	2.5
2	5.0
3	7.5
4	10.0
5	12.5
6	15.0
7	17.5
8	20.5
9	23.0
10	25.5
11	28.0
12	30.5
13	33.0
14	35.5
15	38.0

Temperatures

Fahrenheit	Celsius
32°	0°
212°	100°
250°	120°
275°	140°
300°	150°
325°	160°
350°	180°
375°	190°
400°	200°
425°	220°
450°	230°
475°	240°
500°	260°

Index

Numbers in *italics* refer to photos.